Grounding Motherhood

Healing from the Root

Soon Yoo Anaya Hong

Copyright © 2025 Soon Yoo Anaya Hong

This book contains elements of fiction and creative non-fiction. Certain names, characters, and events have been changed, combined, or dramatized for narrative purposes. Any resemblance to real persons, living or dead, is purely coincidental. All reflections are shared solely from the author's personal perspective.

No part of this book may be reproduced, stored in a retrieval system, or transmitted in any form or by any means, electronic, mechanical, photocopying, recording, or otherwise, without express written permission of the publisher.

All rights reserved

Cover artwork by Briony Beech
@the_briony_beech_illustrates

Today, under the eclipse,
I choose to tell my story—the real one.

The one that begins with devotion
and unfolds into freedom.

This is my story:
a raw and tender portrait of my journey
through the wild terrain of motherhood,
healing, and self-discovery.

What begins as quiet devotion to my children,
with muddy walks, cycling rides, and indulging in good food,
unfolds into something far deeper.

As I reclaim my body through movement and breath,
I begin to reclaim my voice, my joy,
and my sense of self.

Through signs and real-life moments,
shared in the rhythm of seasons and family life,
I emerge.

I didn't abandon motherhood to find freedom.
I found freedom within it.

This is not a story of perfection.
It's a story of barefoot healing.
Of returning to the body.
Of confronting inherited pain.

And I rise. Whole. Powerful. Unfiltered.
The sky closes a cycle today. So do I.

For my children, for being my roots and my wind

CONTENTS

Chapter 1	1
Chapter 2	13
Chapter 3	26
Chapter 4	49
Chapter 5	67
Chapter 6	92
Chapter 7	107
The Witch's Tree	136
Epilogue	139

Preface

Around three years ago, amidst the upheaval of heartbreak and self-discovery, a man moored on Regent's Canal, Merlin, pulled a tarot card and shared a simple yet profound truth: 'Sometimes you have to lose a little to gain a lot.' At the time, those words felt like a bitter pill to swallow.

Becoming a newly single mother of two pushed me into places I had never been. I had to face everything I had once avoided: childhood wounds, toxic patterns, and the echo of my father's presence in the men I had loved. It felt like everything I had constructed around me had to fall away. But in the silence that followed, I began to rebuild. Not from fear. From truth.

Guided by the universe, through songs, numbers, dreams, and cards, I started to listen. I was no longer looking outside myself for validation or permission. I was learning to trust. To surrender. To believe that doing good would bring good. And slowly, I began to receive: unexpected blessings, moments of grace, and a quiet but powerful faith that I was being led. The universe guided me, quietly but consistently. Confirming what my soul had always known. I stopped waiting for someone to choose me. I chose myself.

Grounding Motherhood: Healing from the Root is the story of how I broke free from ancestral patterns, reclaimed my voice, and stepped into my power. And I created space for my children to grow in freedom, truth, and love.

This is what becoming whole looks like: rooted in truth, led by love, and built from within.

I found the woman I was always meant to be.

Rooted. Radiant. Shining brighter than ever.

Chapter 1

Recognising Old Patterns

A year in therapy after a rough breakup helped me uncover patterns I'd carried through most of my life. I began to understand the true nature of my romantic relationships and I was finally able to recognise the undeniable parallels between my ex-partners' behaviours and that of my father. It became painfully clear that the sense of familiarity and dependency I harboured towards Mauricio and Steve was rooted in the resemblance they bore to my own father and a deep sense within me of inadequacy and fear.

Unknowingly, I had been repeating the same dynamics I had witnessed between my father and my mother. Just as my father would undermine my mother and hold financial control, I found myself depending on my ex-partners in similar ways, placing their needs above my own and sacrificing my self worth. This unspoken sense of hierarchy, where I was taught to believe that men were more important, had been ingrained in me for years. And although the relationships developed in different ways, there was always a power struggle dynamic present between me and Mauricio, and then with Steve.

The similarities were becoming increasingly clear. They all shared a certain charisma, a charm that projected an image of respectability and success. They carried themselves with confidence and had built reputations that others often admired. But beneath the surface lay a constructed persona: carefully curated façades of generosity and charm, with public displays of kindness that subtly served to reinforce their control or enhance their image, rather than genuinely helping others. I recall instances where they suggested grandiose gestures, or made bold statements based on their perceived superiority. Mauricio often justified his actions with his nationality, while my father would boast about his appearance, often disguising belittling remarks as 'jokes' to undermine others. With Steve, it wasn't just about helping or giving, it was about making sure people knew he had helped. And yet, behind closed doors, it was like he barely registered what anyone else needed.

Looking back, I recall vividly the demeaning behaviour my father showed towards my mother, often mocking her in front of my sister and me. Her exotic looks, initially a source of admiration, were now being used to mock my mother and explain her inadequacy and sudden emotional reactions. This pattern of belittlement and reactive behaviour echoed in my relationships, where my partners consistently undermined my self-worth, making me feel frustrated and misunderstood.

Steve's flirtatious nature and a tendency to be dismissive created an environment where I was constantly doubting myself. He would hide our family pictures while I was away with the kids to bring women into our home. I remember being told by neighbours and our dog walker of what was happening. One time I asked Steve about a turquoise scrub that was left in our shower, he said it belonged to 'Carl', his accountant. Something didn't feel right. I remember offering Steve to have an open relationship—there was a time I would have done anything for him. But that day, just like the others, Steve labelled my concerns as mere figments of my imagination. He would often go as far as discrediting me in front of others or accuse other people of wanting to cause drama in our relationship.

His refusal to take responsibility for his actions only added to the emotional toll, twisting my responses to validate his claims of instability. I found myself doubting my own reality, and continuously struggling to establish firm boundaries and advocate for myself.

In my family, my father's disloyalty manifested in how late he would get home each night, and in his mysterious work trips, which later unveiled his infidelity. It is not a surprise that we never addressed these concerns openly at home. After discovering my father's infidelity with a woman half his age, he packed his belongings the same day and left the family home. For years after that, he was allowed to walk into our house without notice 'because he was providing for us'.

Just as my father's disloyalty shattered my family and led to his abrupt departure, Steve's betrayal followed a similar script. Steve left after hastily gathering his belongings in the wake of my discovery of damning text messages. He then continued to assert his presence in my life, showing up whenever it suited him. In the aftermath, he inflicted a deeper wound by callously dismissing my hurt, both physically and emotionally. The day after he left, I sent him the pictures of the bruises he had caused on my arms, my legs, and my hips when he was trying to get his phone back, and explained that it was too painful for me to take our five month baby in the carrier. Steve simply sent me three hundred pounds, half of the rent, and offered to help with our son for the next few days 'as long as I didn't cause him any trouble and let him move on with his life alone'. Everything changed. Almost as if a mask had been removed. Steve's refusal to acknowledge his actions, let alone offer an apology shattered my world to the ground.

The echoes of my father's actions reverberated in my second relationship, leaving me grappling with a sense of déjà vu. It was as though history was repeating itself, and I found myself once again confronted with the painful aftermath of deceit and abandonment. When my father left, he sought refuge in a house he intended to refurbish, and some time later, his lover had moved in with him. His actions remained unchecked, leaving my mother, my sister and myself to navigate the pain of abandonment and unacknowledged hurt. Ironically, Steve also moved into a house he had recently purchased for renovation. Like my father, Steve's approach seemed to rely on time to serve as an apology, as if the passage of years could somehow erase the wounds inflicted. They both chose indifference over accountability, leaving me to confront the shattered remnants of trust and self-worth, longing for acknowledgment and closure.

Just like my father, Steve was very intentional about the image he projected to others. He carefully curated a public persona of generosity and charm, but underneath, it was often a way to maintain control. One of the clearest examples was the way he built a circle of people whose loyalty depended on him financially. His closest friends weren't just confidants, they were also his employees. Whenever he met someone new, he was quick to offer grand gestures, creating an emotional bond that usually came with tangible rewards. It was generosity with strings attached. By tying people's well-being to his approval, he ensured a kind of silent obedience.

In the beginning, I had a good relationship with the people from his company. But that changed the moment I asked for their support, not for me, but for our son. When compassion no longer aligned with their financial interests, they all blocked me. Every single one of them, except for our son's godparents. Their loyalty wasn't to me, nor to Steve, but to their godson. Everything they did was guided by one question: What is best for him? And for that, I will always be grateful.

While I longed for an apology and a sense of accountability, Steve chose a path that seemed to avoid confrontation and reflection. Where I sought to make sense of my past and heal through understanding, he appeared to retreat into a place of emotional distance, prioritising self-reliance over connection. Raised in an environment where instability was normalised and vulnerability was discouraged, perhaps emotional detachment became a survival mechanism. Perhaps discarding people when they were no longer useful became a pattern, shaped by his mother's unpredictable absences, often linked to relationships outside the marriage. Recognising this allows me to approach our dynamics with more empathy and understand that his choices may speak to the lasting effects of his childhood experiences too.

Just as Steve's early experiences may have influenced his view of connection, I've come to see how my own childhood shaped my understanding of romantic relationships and the role I thought I was meant to play within them. There was a strong, unspoken notion that men set the terms, and women adapted to them, often trading personal freedoms for the security of the family. I remember my mother, always saving the best-looking or largest portion for my father, a small, but telling gesture that seemed to convey her role in ensuring his comfort above all else. More telling, perhaps, is that in the fifteen years my parents were together, I can't recall a single time she went out with friends on her own, without taking us kids along. Her entire world, it seemed, was bound to our family. These memories reveal the quiet but profound sacrifices she made, and I see now how they influenced my own expectations: how I equated love with sacrifice and worth with selflessness.

As I began to unravel these deeply embedded beliefs, I sought ways to heal the emotional wounds they left behind. I started with a purge with Kambo, to cleanse myself of the negative energy that had been holding me back for so long. After the session, the healer suggested I pull an oracle card while she made me a smoothie. Among the many options she laid out, the card I pulled was the 'Anchor to Fly' card, a symbol of rising up to meet my destiny. What surprised me most was how the woman in the image looked so much like me, her skin tone, her black eyes, even her nose, holding the hand of a little girl who was flying. 'Maybe it is your children that will take you to new heights,' Claire said. That moment felt like a sign from the universe, a confirmation that I was ready to embrace the path ahead.

After that, my first Reiki session with Cat marked a turning point, bringing a sense of peace and clarity that deepened the shift within me. Cat revealed that my past relationships had taken a toll on my throat and solar plexus chakras, the centres of communication and self-worth.

I had spent years swallowing my pain, silencing my truth, and minimising my needs to avoid conflict or rejection. I let things slide, things that weren't fair, weren't kind, weren't right. I tolerated disrespect in the name of love or peace, and in doing so, I handed others permission to cross boundaries I hadn't yet learned to protect.

I actually noticed a curious pattern during my meals with Steve. Every evening, without fail, I would clumsily spill food on myself while seated on the couch in front of the TV. It wasn't until later that I realised the significance of this seemingly mundane occurrence. It dawned on me that this physical manifestation was a reflection of a deeper issue: a lack of alignment with my third chakra, Manipura, the chakra associated with self-worth and personal power. Interestingly, after the relationship ended, I noticed that these spills ceased to happen. It was as though breaking free from that dynamic allowed me to realign with my true sense of self and restore the personal power I had unknowingly surrendered.

I remember when Cat pulled out the Knight of Swords during the first tarot reading, revealing an immense mission that the universe had entrusted to me: to break free from the cycles that had trapped not just me, but generations of women before me in my family. That I had to reshape my future as a woman, and the future of other women in my family—including my daughter's.

The enormity of that message felt almost impossible to grasp, yet with each passing day, it proved itself to be undeniable for the universe was determined to test and reveal my resilience. Forcing me to confront the parts of myself I'd been avoiding: my insecurities, the beliefs that held me back, and the patterns I'd internalised. It was a process of deconstructing who I thought I was and rebuilding something stronger, something aligned with the life I wanted to create.

◆ ◆ ◆

Chapter 2

Unearthing Insecurities

For decades, I felt a profound disconnect from my true self. The negative narrative that I continuously gave myself dictated my perception of the world. I was pretending in front of others, desperately trying to fit in, buried beneath layers of shame and fear of inadequacy. I crafted an image of myself based on how I believed others judged me, struggling to identify my own needs and desires amidst the noise. Upon reflection, I discovered that my insecurities began to take root during my school years. Despite excelling academically, I was often mocked for the difficulty others had pronouncing my name and the shape of my eyes.

These early experiences of feeling different fuelled a deep yearning to belong, which only intensified as I grew older. I remember idolising girls with lighter skin, taller or simply 'prettier', who seemed so effortlessly confident and polished. They came from elite schools that didn't even exist in my hometown and spoke of far-off places I could only dream of visiting. Around them, I became hyper-aware of my differences and tried to mould myself into whatever I thought would help me fit in. I faked interests, adjusted my behaviour, and went out of my way to be accommodating, desperate for their acceptance. My constant self-doubt left me questioning every interaction—had I been likeable enough? Had I somehow let the

m down? This cycle of insecurity and self-neglect left me frustrated, unproductive, and even more disconnected from myself.

My appearance became a double-edged sword, drawing both unwelcome criticism and unwanted attention. I remember when my aunt enrolled me in a coding course when I was in the last year of primary school. It was part of the growing excitement around this new phenomenon called the internet. I enjoyed the lessons and felt I had talent for it. However, my experience was tainted by unsettling encounters. On my way to class every Saturday morning, I often passed a man who would persistently try to start conversations, asking for my name or making comments that left me uncomfortable. One morning, I witnessed something deeply inappropriate that left me shaken: a neighbour behaving inappropriately in plain view of passers-by. I was too young to fully understand, but the sight filled me with unease and fear. Even in the classroom, an older classmate frequently made unwelcome remarks about my appearance and tried to flirt with me, ignoring the fact that I was just a child. Over time, these experiences drained my enthusiasm. I eventually made up an excuse to stop attending the course, feeling a mix of relief and guilt for letting my aunt down. I never told anyone the true reason I skipped that course.

Outside the computing course, dozens of uncomfortable experiences with men followed me throughout much of my life, shaping how I viewed the world and my place within it. In my town, name-calling and crude comments were often brushed off as harmless jokes, but behind them lay a deeply rooted macho mentality that normalised disrespect towards women. As I grew older, I began to experience that culture more intensely. I remember once at the market, I was carrying a cake with both hands when a stranger grabbed my thigh from beneath my skirt as I walked past. On a holiday, a surfing instructor, who was supposed to teach me how to surf, used it as an excuse to touch me inappropriately while we were in the sea. Another time, a man touched me in a swimming pool just because I was next to him. Each time, I felt trapped and voiceless, and a deep sense of shame began to take root inside me.

For a long time, it was hard for me to say no. The only time I remember taking clear action was when, as a teenager, I made all the arrangements to have an abortion. I was absolutely certain of my decision and didn't want anyone else to decide for me. But even then, judgement found its way back to me. When my parents eventually confronted me about their suspicions, my father mentioned hearing rumours about 'my reputation' in the neighbourhood. His words cut deeply, feeding the insecurities I was already carrying.

A few months later, something inside me completely broke. When I innocently opened the family computer, I found photos of my dad having sex with another woman. One image, in particular, was deeply disturbing and has haunted me ever since. Even now, twenty years later, I can still see it as clearly as the day I found it—her eyes staring straight at me. That image refuses to fade, surfacing in my mind at the most unexpected moments and filling me with the same disgust and shame I felt back then. When I showed the pictures to my mum, she rang my dad at work, and within an hour, he was back home. He admitted, without shame or remorse, that he had been with more than twenty women over the past ten years. That same day, he left our home, and just a few months later, his lover had moved in with him. My mum was devastated by his betrayal and his absence. In her pain, she once told me she wished I had never shown her the photos. I felt ashamed and guilty, as though I were the one responsible for their separation.

About a year later, I moved to another city for university. During one of his first visits, my dad brought his girlfriend along. There was something oddly familiar about her, though I couldn't immediately place it. Days later, I confronted them. At first, they denied everything, but eventually admitted she was the woman from the photos. I was furious. I asked him to end the relationship, but of course, he didn't. He simply expected everyone to accept it.

Over time, he began to speak openly about their trips, even though he knew we had previously been lied to. He would mention how she had accompanied him on all those so-called 'work trips' and 'events.' It became clear that he had been living a double life for years, and that his colleagues had not only known about it, but accepted it as normal. Suddenly, things began to make sense. My dad's friends were always the same, but the women changed: wives would come to family holidays and birthday parties, while completely different women, their lovers, were present at work. I recall feeling confused during a family trip when I was about ten, because I was sure the women all looked different. The two lives were kept separate, but I had seen both without understanding it at the time.

All of his friends, who called themselves "la chamaquiza"—the youngsters—were having affairs with much younger women, usually assistants fresh out of university, while still keeping their official wives at home. Whenever I questioned that reality, my dad would become cold and distant. But even so, I still craved his love and approval, so I ended up giving in. I even apologised to his girlfriend for having rejected her before.

A short time after introducing their relationship, my dad told us that his girlfriend was pregnant. My half-sister, nearly thirty years younger than me, was on her way. After she was born, my dad would sometimes ask my mum to help look after his child, bringing her to our home so he and his partner could have some time to themselves. I couldn't understand why my mum would help them, but then I was deeply moved by my mum's quiet kindness and generosity when she said to me, 'That child is innocent...'

With each experience, I began to normalise many harmful behaviours from men. Without realising it, I had learnt to stay quiet, to endure, and to adapt, believing that this was what was expected of me. Especially when it came to men. I remember when a university professor told me he had been approved to be my dissertation supervisor. I felt excited and reached out to shake his hand to thank him, but instead of shaking my hand, he kissed me on the lips. I froze, pulled away, and left immediately. I called my mum to tell her what had happened. To my surprise, she told me to be "nice" to him, to just go along with it. She saw him as a powerful figure at the university, someone who could open doors for me.

I felt confused, disgusted, but also guilty for making a fuss. Little by little, I began to convince myself that maybe this was just part of the price I had to pay to move forward. That if this gave me opportunities, I should try to bear it. So when he called to apologise, I told him not to worry. I acted understanding. And just like that, without even realising it, we started a relationship. He was sixty-four, and I was twenty-two.

That relationship, like many others, left me with a confusing mix of power and emptiness. I started to realise it wasn't the first time I had acted based on what others expected of me. If I'm being honest, since I was a child, I thought I knew how to read people, how to say what they wanted to hear and do what they wanted me to do. In my mind, anything was valid as long as it earned their approval. I was far too concerned with how others saw me, depending on their acceptance to feel validated. It became a compulsion to present a flawless façade, tirelessly trying to be liked.

Although I told myself I was being generous, offering help and attention was, in reality, a subtle way of trying to control people's reactions. To get something in return. I felt that if they liked me, I'd feel better about myself. This realisation was both painful and liberating. Slowly, I began to understand that the only things I could truly control were my own thoughts, feelings, and actions. I had to learn how to build my sense of worth from within, rather than forcing others to meet my emotional needs. It was a hard truth to swallow, but it marked the beginning of my healing journey.

I realised that pretty much my whole life I have been restricted by my own narrative of not being worthy. I spent a lot of time worrying about how others perceived me, beating myself down and feeling like an imposter. I noticed the tendency of undermining myself after receiving a compliment: I would immediately point out something negative about myself instead of simply saying 'thank you'. It's almost like I didn't believe the light that was within me. I was sure that my value was external, brought by someone else but me.

I kept limiting and underplaying myself. Sabotaging my own life, convinced that someone had to rescue me. I remember how easily I used to become overwhelmed and get trapped in moments of self-doubt and second-guessing myself. I would suddenly doubt my own decisions and sabotage my actions out of fear and insecurity. Many times, I would panic and make choices against my instincts. Simple choices like deciding between taking the bus or the underground became paralysing decisions. Negative thoughts and incessant overthinking became my unwelcome companions.

Jealousy became a shadow that loomed over my relationships, intertwined with my deep-seated insecurities and fear of not being enough for my partners. The slightest glance towards other women or the veil of secrecy surrounding their consumption of pornography would ignite a storm of doubt within me, deepening my feelings of inadequacy. Steve's constant flirting with other women only served to exacerbate these insecurities, leaving me questioning my own worth and desirability. Despite my instincts warning me of Steve's infidelities, I chose to ignore the signs, clinging to the hope of salvaging the relationship out of a paralysing fear of loneliness.

After our final break up, the sense of injustice and cruelty felt overwhelming, prompting incessant replays of past events in my mind. I grappled with the need to validate my pain, seeking acknowledgment and an apology from Steve. Long, impassioned messages poured from my fingertips, each word an attempt to justify my worthiness of respect and recognition. Yet, despite my efforts, my pleas fell on deaf ears, dismissed as the outbursts of an emotionally volatile individual. My emotional turmoil was perceived as a lack of control, a failure to regulate my emotions.

I found myself engulfed in a whirlwind of feelings, unable to break free from the grip of obsession. Every waking moment was consumed by thoughts of Steve, agonising over his perception of me and yearning for his validation. Despite the pain he inflicted upon my heart, I remained tethered to the hope that he would reach out, that he would offer some semblance of closure or reconciliation. Reluctant to see my own worth, I kept thinking that only through him I could be happy.

When he left, I was only inclined to prepare a nice meal if my kids were around, otherwise, I would just have a cup of tea and binge eat biscuits or just make a piece of toast. I went down two sizes in a few months and even my friends were worried about my weight loss. It was an unconscious act, rooted in the belief I was not worth the effort. With him gone, I did not even know what to get for dessert, and generally doubted what I liked. Deciding what to watch on Netflix was simply a waste of time because I could not make up my mind. It was as if my whole identity had left with him. Now, I can see the depth of my co-dependency, seeking in him a sense of who I was.

◆◆◆

Chapter 3

Romantic Relationships

Instead of facing the inadequacy of my relationships, I always clung to them with a desperate determination, refusing to let go even when the cracks became undeniable. I remember the endless cycles of breakups and reconciliations, the explosive arguments followed by equally intense reunions that felt like a fleeting balm for deeper wounds. Passion and chaos became intertwined, and I mistook the highs and lows for love. I convinced myself that the turbulence was normal, even inevitable, as if enduring it proved my worth. It wasn't just the relationships I was holding on to, it was the belief that I needed someone else to complete me, to fill the void left by the insecurities and doubts I carried like a second skin.

Like in many other homes in Mexico and across Latin America, I grew up with the belief that only men were the providers of material goods, while women were meant to sacrifice themselves, exhaust their energy, and neglect their own well-being for the sake of others. Women were expected to clean, care for the children, cook, and work, all without taking time for themselves. This mentality made me feel limited simply for being a woman.

I never imagined that I could bring wealth or success into my life on my own terms. Instead, I expected men to be the ones to provide those things, but at the same time, I was bracing myself for them to disappoint me. I expected them to be my saviours, but in the end, they always ended up taking advantage of me. And in a way, I emotionally detached, adopting a "whatever" attitude, telling myself I didn't care, even though deep down I was carrying the weight of shame. Shame that I wasn't enough. Because I had been let down by my father and by practically every man I've ever known, and my subconscious kept making me relive that pain through the constant feeling that I was never going to be valued the way I deserved.

In hindsight, I can see how I was drawn to relationships that mirrored the pattern I'd learned from my father. I had been conditioned to expect men to be emotionally distant or unpredictable, and without realising it, I sought out partners who reflected that same behaviour. It was as though I was recreating the dynamics of my childhood, unconsciously trying to resolve the feelings of hurt and abandonment my father had left me with. It was shocking to recognise how much I had romanticised rejection. I even changed the ringtone to the cavalry whenever Steve contacted me, because it felt like such a rare occasion that it had to be announced in a special way. A text here, a fleeting moment of attention there, was just enough to give me this high or comfort that would later disappear and I would seek that relief again and again. An insidious bond quietly took hold, its invisible threads weaving through moments of affection and despair.

Over time, that constant need to feel valued, comforted, or simply not alone led me, from a very young age, into relationships that were rushed, intense, or even unsafe. My expectations of love were shaped by narrow ideas, romanticised by the telenovelas we used to watch and by cultural notions that a woman's worth depended on how well she could cook, how pleasing she could be, or how much she could endure. Life would be very hard and unfair for her, but just by being beautiful, some man would come to rescue her and lift her out of poverty. That's how it was shown over and over again in the telenovelas, and that's what I started to believe.

Although my mom always had a full-time job, and sometimes even two, she was never the one who bought us clothes or gave us luxuries. I always had the impression that we had to sacrifice a lot in order to have money, and that only my father could give us those extras. When I was a child, during the week my dad used to be away, 'at work', all day long, and would come home late at night. But on the weekends, he would always drive us to the shopping mall, we'd have a nice dinner with him, and get new clothes. Those gestures felt like proof of worthiness, a temporary salve for his absence. I came to view love as grand gestures and dramatic emotions. Mauricio and Steve were no exception, though the way that intensity unfolded with each of them was uniquely their own.

With Mauricio, it was as though we were caught in a whirlwind from the start. We met traveling in Central America, and within ten days, we were engaged, promising each other forever before we'd even begun to really know one another. At the time, it felt electric: a connection so undeniable that it seemed only natural to make a lifetime commitment so quickly. It didn't occur to me to question the speed or to wonder whether we were rushing into something neither of us fully understood. My father was the only one who hesitated, openly expressing concern about Mauricio. But I brushed it off, convinced that no one else could see the depth of what we had. My friends were also surprised by the announcement of our engagement but I ignored their warnings too, same as all the red flags that appeared. We got married four months later and in two weeks I left Mexico with Mauricio to live in Europe with him.

With Steve, though it didn't feel as rushed, the relationship was just as intense, marked by grand gestures and emotional highs that were hard to escape. Meeting him felt like recognition, as though we were two pieces of the same puzzle finally clicking into place. But then I came to realise that there was a sense of ease in both relationships, we used to say, 'We're a perfect match.' I can't help but question where that belief came from. Was it because I was so eager to please, bending to their desires to make sure I was chosen? Or was it because I saw something in them that reminded me of my dad? Maybe it was a mix of both. Something in them felt familiar, like an emotional shortcut to a sense of safety, even though that sense of safety wasn't really there. I told myself we were perfect for each other and that I was the one they needed. Now I see how much I sought out that intensity, mistaking it for love. I equated passion with depth, urgency with certainty, and commitment with validation. It's only now that I can step back and recognise how those feelings often blurred my ability to see the reality of my relationships.

To my surprise, I've discovered that both relationships followed a clear and painful cycle. In the beginning, Steve and Mauricio seemed to embody my dreams, almost as if they had taken my deepest desires and reflected them back to me. There were grand gestures, flattering words, and a whirlwind of attention that made me feel special, cherished and desired. Steve, for example, once spoke about us living in the wilderness in Central America, where I could pursue my passion for research, exactly the dream I had given up when married Mauricio and left my country. It was the ultimate promise: not just a life together but the opportunity to reclaim the career and identity I had sacrificed. Similarly, Mauricio started with grand gestures, like carrying a massive cake up a mountain for my birthday, planning every detail with care. But over time, those gestures disappeared. Steve's initial thoughtful,

Everything was part of a greater plan: a journey my soul was destined to take. When I was at university, I remember feeling an inexplicable pull towards London. I even inquired about studying here, but the cost made it impossible at the time. But I was always meant to end up here: in London. To see my children grow, to provide a safe home for them. This is where I was meant to break free from the burdens of my past, and step into my highest self.

Living with Mauricio and meeting Steve were difficult but necessary parts of my transformation. They reflected back my deepest insecurities, fears, and triggers. And only by being in relationship with them was I able to truly recognise the patterns I was unconsciously choosing. Patterns rooted in survival, in seeking approval, and in not believing I deserved more.

But once I saw them clearly, I began choosing differently—consciously. Not from fear, but from self-awareness. Not to please, but to honour my truth.

expensive gifts became afterthoughts, and Mauricio eventually forgot my birthday altogether.

The magic never lasted. Gradually, their attention and affection faded, replaced by subtle criticisms or dismissals. I became acutely aware of how my needs were overlooked, but I convinced myself that if I tried harder, things would return to how they once were. In both relationships, there was a pattern that initially made me feel deeply valued but later left me questioning my self-worth. With Mauricio, he often bragged about me in the early days, telling people how lucky he was to be with someone so accomplished and beautiful. But over time, the admiration faded and I suddenly became a 'Mexican't' to his eyes. His 'jokes' constantly chipped away at my sense of self-worth. It was painful to feel that the admiration I once inspired had turned into criticism and indifference. The emotional detachment before our relationship ended became undeniable. Mauricio no longer made any effort to be kind; after six years being together, when I suggested taking a break, his response, 'I'm not going to beg you', was a chilling dismissal of everything we had shared.

With Steve, the dynamic was different but equally disheartening. Early on, he told me how much he valued my insights and support, saying he felt comfortable sharing his ideas with me and that I was like his partner in everything. I felt seen and appreciated in ways I hadn't before. But as time passed, the closeness faded. He stopped including me in his plans, started doing things behind my back, and became distant. I kept looking for his approval all the time. But when our son was born, the balance of attention shifted. My focus naturally turned toward our child, and it became clear that what I could offer emotionally and practically no longer satisfied Steve. He started to be so mean to me, that unconsciously I started to associate Steve with Mauricio, I had to stop myself many times from calling him that name by accident.

Steve also became obsessed with the idea of travelling. He would plan 'business' trips or visits to see his mother or friends, without telling me where he was going or when he'd be back. That growing distance also started to show in our intimacy. At first, there was mutual attraction and connection, but toward the end, I felt increasingly rejected. Whenever I tried to initiate closeness, he would either ignore me or say he just wasn't in the mood. I later found out that he preferred watching pornography or seeking connections with his employees and collaborators.

Eventually, I discovered that during those solo trips, he had been living a parallel life in the countries he travelled to. That's why he had always resisted the idea of taking us with him. I remember him saying that the 'altitude wouldn't be good for the baby', and that's why he needed to go away alone for weeks at a time.

After we had already separated, the power play became even more obvious. The first time he went on a trip alone, he came to pick up our son wearing a T-shirt with the name of a city and its exact coordinates. It felt like a mockery, a calculated gesture meant to remind me that he was still in control, as if he still needed to assert his power over me.

Our inside jokes, the things we used to enjoy together, and that feeling of being in sync suddenly disappeared. I couldn't understand how everything that once connected us, from small affinities to shared values and future goals, had vanished. I replayed the moments over and over in my head, wondering what I had done wrong or how I had misread things. I kept trying to make sense of what was happening.

The pain of feeling unwanted and abandoned became overwhelming. The more I craved Steve's validation, the deeper I sank into a sea of doubt and insecurity. I became a kind of detective in my own life, analysing every interaction in detail, searching for clues of betrayal. And even when I found clear signs, I was met with a chorus of denial and gaslighting that slowly eroded my sense of reality.

I remember how Steve's secrecy around his business trips and friends used to be in the back of my mind all the time, fearing the worst and fuelling my anxiety. My therapist astutely observed that my breaths were shallow and frequent, and he suggested that my body was perpetually high on cortisol due to my constant state of fight or flight throughout that tumultuous relationship. This chronic stress kept me on edge all the time, so when a decision was required or something unexpected happened, I would easily become overwhelmed. I often second-guessed myself and made panicked choices that didn't work out, which left me feeling even more frustrated and in a bad mood around my kids.

That emotional toll was made even heavier by a constant sense of loss. Whether through outright rejection or emotional neglect, these experiences were very difficult to process. The shifts with Mauricio and Steve, from feeling admired and cherished to feeling rejected and unseen, left me holding on, trying to recapture what had been so intoxicating at the start. It was as though I was clinging to the promise of who they had been in the beginning, hoping that person would return.

This stage was the hardest to endure, and it also brought to light the darkest side of me. Anger and despair consumed me in both relationships. The constant frustration of being unseen and unheard led to moments where my emotions spilled over. I would lash out or react in ways that made me feel ashamed afterward. These outbursts felt like they came from a place I didn't recognise, as though I was no longer in control of my emotions.

Anger and frustration often boiled beneath the surface between me and Mauricio. We constantly engaged in unnecessary fights, and genuine communication and understanding were nearly impossible between us. His 'jokes' would usually lead to uncomfortable moments with strangers and friends and I really wondered if he lacked the ability to connect with other people's feelings. Despite my attempts to express myself, I found myself repeatedly unheard and dismissed. The frustration grew to such an extent that I felt compelled to record our conversations, desperate to prove the validity of my feelings. However, my efforts were met with gaslighting and denial, leaving me feeling constantly invalidated and powerless.

Bursts of frustration became a daily occurrence, and I felt trapped in an unrelenting cycle of pain and helplessness. This emotional toll began manifesting physically: constant tension in my jaw, especially at night so I had to wear teeth guards to sleep, and chronic back pain for years. Despite regular physiotherapy and acupuncture sessions the pain never truly went away. It wasn't until I finally left Mauricio that the pain miraculously subsided, as though my body had been holding onto the anguish I couldn't release. Years of suppressed anger, frustration, and resentment had quietly settled in my body. Over time, I've come to understand that these emotions are deeply human. With practice and self-compassion, I've learned to notice the signs and triggers that indicate I'm becoming emotionally dysregulated. Most importantly, I've gained the ability to regulate my responses. In the past, my shoulders would tense up, and a tingling sensation would climb my spine as emotions surged through me. It felt like a wave of heat flooding my body, a physical expression of the rage I couldn't name. A force that, at the time, felt impossible to contain.

Looking back, I can now see how similar my experiences are to what my mother endured in her own relationship. She, too, reached breaking points after years of suppression and emotional exhaustion, reacting in ways that were a natural response to being pushed beyond her limits. At the time, I didn't understand her reactions. My dad would dismiss them, attributing her behaviour to a 'bad temper' or claiming her way of 'understanding' or 'seeing' things was different from ours because of her nationality. But her reactions were the result of enduring immense emotional pressure without any healthy release.

The constant psychological manipulation shattered my sense of reality and eroded my self-esteem. I often found myself questioning whether I was too sensitive or overreacting to Mauricio and Steve's behaviour. I remember a simple incident with coffee: Mauricio made me a cup, and it tasted so bitter that

I kept adding sugar, yet when I pointed out the odd flavour, he explained that instead of throwing out the water from the hot water bottle I'd used the night before, he thought I would appreciate it if he wasn't wasteful. It didn't make sense to me, but he insisted it was perfectly normal. Moments like this made me second-guess myself, unsure of what was real or right.

Even in more direct confrontations, I felt dismissed by Mauricio. I asked him not to raise his voice at me, and when I used a decibel meter to measure how loud he was during an argument, he dismissed it, claiming the numbers were wrong. The constant invalidation and lack of emotional consideration had a devastating impact on me, leading to such a deep depression that I even attempted to take my own life.

I lived with a constant heaviness, as if something was weighing me down, making it hard to breathe. I was on antidepressants for months and tried to stay active, keeping my mind occupied with a part-time job and looking after my daughter. A few months later, I got a full-time job as a science teacher at

School 21. I remember one day, just a couple of weeks after I had started, I was waiting for the bus with my daughter when an older woman approached me and, to my surprise, spoke in my mother tongue: '¿Ya te divorciaste?' ('Are you divorced yet?'). Her question caught me off guard. I hesitated before responding, instinctively assuring her that everything was fine. As I slipped my hand into my pocket, my fingers brushed against a coin. Without thinking, I pulled it out and handed it to her. It was a shiny two-pound coin. She accepted it with a nod and said, 'Your daughter will have good fortune,' before walking away. That brief encounter lingered in my mind.

I begged Mauricio to leave, so I could stay home with my daughter, but he told me that if we separated, I would lose my right to remain in the country because my visa depended on him, and that I might not see our daughter again. At the time, I believed him. I had no reason to think he would lie about something so serious. I felt doomed: if I wanted to be near my daughter, I had to stay with Mauricio.

At work, I was in an environment completely different from what I was living through at home. I was surrounded by people who genuinely cared about their students, loved learning, and generously shared their knowledge. They were happy to see others shine and helped them shine too. I felt seen and respected, not just as a teacher, but as a scientist, a mother, and as a whole person. Being there reminded me of who I really was beneath all the exhaustion and self-doubt I had been carrying. It was the first time in years that I began to recognise my own worth again.

At School 21, there was a genuine culture of celebrating each other's achievements and offering both praise and constructive feedback. People were deeply interested in each other's personal and professional growth, and that mindset made all the difference. I was especially lucky to have wonderful mentors and supportive colleagues in the science department, who made me feel part of a team where everyone wanted to see each other succeed. That sense of community, encouragement, and generosity helped me rebuild my confidence and remember what I was truly capable of.

When my first salary was deposited, I finally found the courage to leave. I knew that if I stayed with Mauricio any longer, I would reach that breaking point again—and this time, I couldn't risk not making it back. Later, I understood that his words had been designed to instil fear in me, to make me feel cornered and dependent. It wasn't until I finally left and asked for legal help that I realised I had the right to stay in the country because of my own merits.

Looking back, I truly believe that the woman at the bus stop was sent to awaken something within me. It was the exact set of conditions my soul needed to begin setting itself free: the combination of unique and shared experiences, the place I found myself in, and the right people around me, all of it allowing me to truly hear that message. A message to grow. To trust myself enough to move forward in my career and to begin imagining a future that was truly my own.

And as I began listening more closely to the quiet whispers of intuition, life began placing the right guides in my path. One memory that stands out is my first-ever tarot card reading shortly after Steve left. A wanderer moored along the Regent's Canal, Merlin, spoke with a calm certainty that I couldn't shake. He told me he could see two relationships in my past but said, 'Well, one and a half, really, because the love was only half.' He also pulled the Star card, and I remember him saying, 'Sometimes, you have to lose a little to gain a lot.' At the time, everything seemed encoded, and I left confused and with even more questions. Little did I know that this would be my first step into a world of synchronicities, signs from the universe, and a deeper understanding of divine plans.

It was as if the universe had been patiently waiting for me to be ready, to open my eyes, my heart, and finally receive. Time showed me that the 'half' wasn't just about my relationships, it was about me. All this time, I hadn't fully loved myself. Letting go of those relationships, along with the beliefs and patterns that had chained me, was painful. But in that loss, I was able to uncover the strength and resilience I hadn't realised I had and rebuilt something far greater. I could trust myself again, relying on my ability to make choices grounded in love and truth, for both myself and my children.

My past relationships taught me hard truths about myself and the power dynamics I allowed to shape my life. I was forced to confront my limits, my fears, and my capacity for growth. And while they marked an ending, they also planted the seeds for a new beginning: one where I could face the challenges of co-parenting with a clearer sense of who I was, and what my children and I deserved.

◆ ◆ ◆

23. ANCHOR TO FLY

Chapter 4

Co-parenting with Two Dads

I have noticed that the patterns of power and influence in both Mauricio and Steve's behaviour are often very similar, which has made it easier for me to see the common threads and better understand these dynamics. Sometimes this showed up through clear financial pressures or more subtle forms of emotional withdrawal, which helped keep an imbalance of power in place. Their strong need to protect their reputations often made it harder to address things openly and acknowledge the reality of their actions.

Mauricio went a step further by making sure that people in his professional and personal circles, including people at our daughter's school, where he used to work, saw me in the worst possible light. Two years after our separation, I found out that the school actually believed I had no parental rights and that I had 'abandoned' my daughter. It was only when I showed them that I did have full parental rights and shared custody that they finally recognised and treated me as an equal parent.

More disturbingly, I recently discovered that for God knows how long, he's been telling our daughter that I did not see her for nine months after her dad and I separated. Nine months. When she mentioned it, she said she knew it couldn't be true, because 'I'd miss her in 24 hours'. I tried to control my anger and calmly helped her see that it was not true. I mentioned the flat I moved into a few weeks after I left, and she remembered it, and even remembered that once she had stayed overnight and that my bicycle got stolen which made her dad very angry the next morning. She also remembered another place, in Rainham, and how we used to get the C2C in the mornings to get all the way to Stratford. Then I showed her an email with all my addresses during the previous years, including those two houses. She could see it for herself. She understood that it wasn't true that I left because 'I didn't want her'.

Steve, on the other hand, took a different approach. He ensured all our mutual friends cut ties with me, even persuading his parents to block me. Even after I showed Steve's parents pictures of the bruises he had caused me the day he moved out, they ignored my message and blocked me immediately. Their reaction, like Steve's own behaviour, revealed a deep unwillingness to acknowledge the truth or offer support.

Mauricio and Steve's calculated actions reflected not only their unwillingness to accept responsibility but also their determination to isolate me, ensuring their versions of events went unchallenged. Steve even went as far as claiming that my insistence on him taking accountability for the pain he caused was 'harassment,' which he used as an excuse to leave the country and fire me from his company.

Co-parenting became a new stage where the dynamics of our past relationships persist in subtle and not-so-subtle ways. The power struggles that once defined our partnerships now unfold in decisions about our children. Their involvement in raising our children often blur the line between shared responsibilities and old control games.

Mauricio's approach became a means of punishing me for leaving, using co-parenting as an opportunity to assert control and maintain dominance. Steve, on the other hand, reacted defensively when I tried to hold him accountable. His lack of loyalty and limited involvement with our son became points of tension between us, and instead of facing this, he chose to remain emotionally distant and to avoid the issue altogether.

After I decided to leave Mauricio, I did everything I could to stay involved in our daughter's life, despite the financial and emotional strain. I managed the school runs during the week and spent Sundays with her, doing my best to make those days feel special. To support Mauricio, I continued paying for the Council Tax on their flat for months and even covered the cost of the dog sitter, despite being on an unqualified teacher's salary while he was the head of department. I complied with every rule and restriction he set, as long as it meant I could see my daughter.

At that time, it was very difficult for me to offer my daughter a completely stable home because I had only just separated and was starting from scratch. Even so, I never wanted to lose another minute by her side. I remember how we used to spend our Sundays out, visiting museums, going to the zoo, or simply wandering around the shopping mall, trying to keep the experience joyful and shield her from the reality of my struggles.

The first place I moved into was a box room at a man's house, uncomfortable, but the cheapest option and conveniently around the block from my daughter's home. However, it didn't take long before the man began making unwanted advances, forcing me to move out. But I knew no matter where I lived, even when it had been me who decided to leave, as long as I remained invested and committed to our daughter, Mauricio could not keep her away.

So, I spent the following months looking for the best environment for her. I spent a few weeks on a friend's couch, rented rooms in shared houses, and stayed with other friends. Always making sure to be there for my daughter and provide a sense of stability in her life. When I moved into a beautiful house by Francis Road in Leyton with a couple of friends, Mauricio commented that he was surprised at how well I was managing, but the way he said it made me feel uncomfortable. It didn't feel like a compliment; it was a reminder that he had never really seen me as capable.

Although the relationship between us was tense, it seemed we were learning how to co-parent, until I filed for divorce. Two weeks later, Mauricio announced his intention to take our daughter abroad, seeking full custody and child maintenance. I obviously refused to let her go. That year, we began a custody battle that cost me more than 80% of my annual income in legal fees, as I had no choice but to hire solicitors to defend my rights and protect our daughter from being taken out of the country. His behaviour escalated. He became harassing, more intimidating and increasingly overbearing.

Mauricio's anger was palpable. Bombarding me with spiteful messages first thing in the morning and showing up unannounced to see if a man was with me. The pick up and drop off times were nerve racking. Every time, I felt the tension and fear he created. One day, I arrived two minutes early for a handover, and he refused to let our daughter out of the car, stating, 'It's not your time yet.' He seemed desperate to punish me for leaving.

On our daughter's first birthday after we separated, I had organised a party for her at my home. That morning, when Mauricio was supposed to bring her over to spend the weekend with me, he sent me a text saying that our daughter had a fever and that it would be 'highly unacceptable' to expose other children to a potential illness. He refused to bring her over unless I cancelled the party, due in a few hours. He said that if I didn't cancel the party, he would have to contact each parent directly to tell them that 'their kids would be in danger' if they came to my house. I had no other choice but to cancel the party. The next year Mauricio tried the exact same trick, but when I asked him for proof of our daughter's high temperature, it miraculously disappeared. So, this time we were able to celebrate with her friends.

But the custody battles were even more distressing. He called me to a café one morning and showed me a document he had written, where he named himself our daughter's main carer, set some restrictions on who could enter my home, and where we could go on holiday. He insisted that if I didn't sign there and then, I might not see my daughter again after their holiday trip that winter. 'It would be a shame,' he said. He would often make up his own laws, misuse official orders, distort documents or add clauses of his own that had never been agreed, but that he wanted to impose as rules.

His attempts to control the situation also came through in how he repeatedly distorted facts. He would selectively use details to create a narrative that portrayed me as an unfit and uncaring mother. One evening, he arrived unannounced at my door with another man, demanding that I take a drug test on the spot. I felt I had no choice but to comply. I peed in a plastic cup that he had brought, and he tested it himself, the results were negative. It was a way to intimidate me, to undermine me as a mother, and ultimately, to keep control over me. It was all part of a pattern that repeated itself over and over again: manipulation, pressure, and abuse of power disguised as care or responsibility.

In an attempt to isolate me, Mauricio also tried to turn people in our circle against me, pushing them to choose a side. I remember when Troy, a Mexican friend, showed up as a 'witness' to collect the urine sample that Mauricio wanted. I also noticed how some of the mums from the school no longer wanted to bring their daughters to play at my house, and how it was said that staff at our daughter's school believed I had given up my parental rights. Even an old friend provided a written statement to confirm that I supposedly wanted our daughter to go abroad with her father. Mauricio even called the police twice to have our daughter removed from my home, claiming she was in danger. I still remember the shock of seeing the officers knocking on my door, not knowing what was happening. On both occasions, the officers apologised, confirmed there was no real reason to intervene, and made it clear to me that everything had been deliberately distorted by Mauricio to justify his calls.

But when the time came, I felt truly blessed to have a fair judge who looked at the bigger picture and recognised the imbalance that had affected my relationship with our daughter all that time. Back then, granting joint custody helped protect my place in our daughter's life and ensured that the care, love and stability I could offer her would not simply be taken away.

During the custody battle with Mauricio, Steve was a vital source of support. His financial contributions helped cover part of the legal expenses, and I was grateful for the stability he provided during such a challenging time. Similarly, when I faced the decision of whether to return to my full-time job after my maternity leave, Steve assured me that he would take care of our family and encouraged me to quit my job. Trusting his word, I made the difficult decision to leave my cherished full-time permanent job and focus on our growing family.

After our son was born, Steve employed me through his company, offering me a title and a salary for nearly a year. This arrangement seemed to reflect his commitment to supporting us, but it also placed me in a position of financial dependence. But after his abrupt departure, everything changed. Steve transformed into someone unrecognisable: a figure of cruelty and vindictiveness, whose actions inflicted harm on our family. He fired me from his company and replaced my salary with child maintenance payments. This change left me entirely dependent on him to pay the rent and cover our essential needs. It also meant I was unemployed. So the monthly payments became a tool for financial control and punishment.

Steve would delay payments if I upset him, and in the worst months, he sent me only a quarter of the money, one day before the rent was due, leaving us unable to pay rent and forcing us to scramble for solutions. We eventually reached a new agreement, which is less than half of what Steve used to provide, and a third of what I used to make as a teacher.

Once again, behind the scenes, I was fighting to maintain a sense of normality for my kids. I tried to keep life comfortable and stable, but inside, I would worry each time a payment was needed. For months we relied on food banks and the winter clothes we needed for our first winter came from a church.

Steve's shift from supportive partner to someone who weaponised financial control revealed a deeper cruelty. The security he had promised me evaporated, leaving our family vulnerable and dependent on the kindness of others. This experience exposed the extent to which financial punishment and emotional neglect became his tools for maintaining power and control over our lives.

Steve's behaviour also evolved into a pattern of emotional neglect and withdrawal, where he repeatedly avoided taking responsibility and being vulnerable. When things became difficult, he withdrew even further. His actions, or rather his inactions, showed the truth in his priorities. Instead of being a partner in co-parenting, he seemed to prioritise his so-called freedom.

For me, it seemed natural that Steve and our son should remain in constant or daily communication, but I came to realise that Steve saw this as pestering and an infringement on his freedom. Any updates I shared about our son were dismissed as unnecessary interference, and my attempts to foster a bond between them were misinterpreted as controlling behaviour. This resistance to closeness might reflect deeper patterns from his past, but understanding this didn't make his emotional absence any less painful.

I remember when Steve informed me that he would no longer keep his phone on at night, saying he had no obligations anymore and could do 'whatever suited him, whenever it suited him'. I kept fooling myself, hoping that he actually cared. But the reality of Steve's detachment became painfully clear when our son was diagnosed with COVID-19 at just a few months old. Instead of offering support, Steve left to visit his mother by the sea, using his own struggles with sleep as an excuse to avoid his responsibilities.

After that, Steve's behaviour became even more frustrating and disrespectful. He would cancel at the last minute, sometimes just a couple of hours before he was meant to pick up our son, saying he felt unwell, only to "miraculously" feel better the next day. He refused to commit to any plan and showed no consideration for the impact his erratic behaviour had on me. It felt as though I had to be permanently available, adapt to his timing, and tolerate whatever he decided.

He would not even show basic manners, he would let me know he was running late only when I was already waiting, and during handovers he would often ignore me completely. His lack of respect for my time, along with his repeated failure to follow through on what we had agreed, made me realise that the only way to bring some stability was to request a court order to define the contact arrangements with our son.

I made it clear to him that if he wasn't willing to respect even the most basic agreements, I would have to take the matter to court to formalise it. Only then were we able to agree on a more consistent contact plan, one that at least allowed me to know in advance when he would be coming. That agreement brought a bit more structure and opened the door to a gradual transition, so they could eventually spend short holidays together.

When our son speaks about Steve, his love for his father is evident, which makes the gaps in communication more confusing for him. This is especially noticeable when his sister visits Mauricio, and our son expresses a desire to see his own dad as well.

Despite these challenges, there are glimmers of progress. This year marked the first time Steve took our son for two consecutive nights, and the joyful remarks our son made afterward, like, 'So much fun at Dad's house', offered reassurance that their time together was meaningful.

However, Steve uses the time he spends with our son to continue the power dynamics we had in our relationship. Even with court-ordered requirements for daily updates when Steve is looking after our son, he often disregards this agreement. On weekends when I don't acquiesce to his demands, I receive no updates, no replies to my messages, and sometimes, not even an acknowledgment that they've been read. This year, the voice note my daughter and I sent to my son for his birthday was not played until the next day. On the weekends I don't 'upset' Steve, he fulfils the minimum obligation, sending a single photo with a blunt 'no health concerns,' rather than a meaningful update. Through our son, I learn about trips to the zoo, gymnastics, or the beach, but the photos Steve sends are carefully curated: close-ups of our son sitting on a chair or having a bath, keeping me intentionally out of the loop.

Each silence feels less like forgetfulness and more like a quiet echo of something unresolved, a need to remind me, or perhaps himself, that the past hadn't truly been laid to rest. And when they've had what he deems 'too much' contact over a few consecutive days, Steve abruptly withdraws, as if needing to reassert some unspoken boundary only he understands. In a twisted way, he begins to ignore my messages, not mine as an individual, but those in which our son asks to speak to him, leaving them unanswered, as if temporarily erasing his presence were his way of restoring balance in his own game of control.

Over time, I came to understand that his actions were not just about parenting, they were about power, and I could no longer allow that power to shape how I showed up for my children. I wonder how much our son perceives the strained dynamic between his dad and me, and how deeply it affects him. Just this week, after not seeing Steve in person for a month, they had a long-awaited trip to Spain planned. On the morning of their departure, when Steve arrived to pick him up, our son suddenly refused to leave the house, insisting he wanted to 'stay home with Mum.' It made me question whether the weekly video calls and two weekends a month they spend together are truly meeting his emotional needs or if the underlying tension is impacting him in ways he cannot yet articulate.

Recognising these challenges has reinforced the importance of legal protections as a source of empowerment. While Mauricio and Steve may try to dismiss or ignore me, the court orders ensure they must acknowledge my rights and requests. This legal backing provides a sense of stability and reassurance, reminding me that my voice is not only valid but also protected.

In the past, I was often on edge, easily frustrated, and reactive, but I quickly realised that thriving in our new circumstances required a different approach. Cultivating calmness and self-assurance became a personal challenge I was determined to meet. I understood that the love, stability, and values I impart to my children will ultimately shape their future far more than any moment of conflict or frustration. This shift in mindset empowered me to navigate co-parenting dynamics with a focus on stability and growth, rather than on the chaos of unresolved emotions.

◆ ◆ ◆

Chapter 5

Finding Strength in Unexpected Places

Contrary to what I had always believed, the answer was in letting go. I realise now that with both Mauricio and Steve, our interactions are easier when I let go of expectations. I've learned to recognise the familiar tactics they use, recognise my own triggers and simply not react. My new focus is on setting boundaries and ensuring my needs are respected, which has made our interactions more manageable and less emotionally charged. I finally stopped the lengthy messages to Mauricio advocating for his understanding, and I also stopped waiting for Steve's messages.

I am also trying to be more forgiving to myself, for the explosive moments I've had, and made my children feel scared. When I told Cat about it, she suggested hitting a pillow while saying 'no,' but I found that the kids were scared by this too, so I tried hitting the couch with a pillow with the excuse of cleaning it every night. It was surprisingly effective in releasing my frustration. This simple act was the first step to recognise the frustration, resentment, and anger I had been caring all this time and seek help for my unprocessed emotions. Reiki has been one of the tools I've turned to, along with techniques like controlled breathing and exercises to ground myself in the moment. Sound ceremonies and simply sitting with grief have allowed me to set my soul free. By letting go of my old self, I entered a new time in my life feeling guided and at peace.

I am now able to recognise the signs that I am becoming dysregulated, and I tell my children that I need a break because I am feeling overwhelmed. By being open, my daughter and I have built a relationship based on trust, compassion and empowerment. In the midst of our intimate conversations, a revelation surfaced: her observation that I appeared happier without Steve. Though initially heartbroken, her words unveiled a newfound sense of freedom within our family dynamic. With this liberation, my daughter flourished, embracing silliness and seeking cuddles with an uninhibited spirit.

This new sense of freedom and empowerment at home has made me feel more capable and proactive in seeking changes in our lives. It has now been four years since the judge granted Mauricio and me shared custody, ensuring that our daughter remained in the same city. But I now realise that circumstances have changed, and adjustments are needed to ensure that her needs are truly being met.

Throughout these years, I felt that Mauricio did benefit financially from the custody arrangements, and that his insistence on asking me for money was a way of maintaining a sense of control. By ensuring that he had just enough additional time with our daughter, two extra nights per month, he was able to claim a technical majority of contact, which allowed him to present himself to the authorities as the primary carer.

Paying him child maintenance did not really bother me, after all, I was the one who had left the family home. I made monthly payments since the day I moved out and only stopped when I became unemployed. Still, he kept pushing for money, often after seeing photos of me on social media or assuming I'd gone back to full-time work at the start of the academic year. Each time, he came with new calculations, assumptions, and eagerness to demand payments again. I tried to explain that I wasn't yet in a position to resume them, while reminding that I continued to support our daughter by buying her clothes, shoes, and anything else she needed, never once asking to split the costs.

I never asked him to reimburse me for the clothes I sent to his home. I knew it was the only way to make sure our daughter always had what she needed throughout the week as she grew. Most times I would just avoid confrontations by not asking him to share the costs but every year, when it was time to get a new uniform, he would suggest a ten-pound shoe allowance and insisted on covering only half of what I spent, comparing it to prices at Asda or Primark, even when I had not bought from these shops. I can't help but cringe when he talks like that, but I choose to stay focused on giving our daughter what she needs.

The last time he asked for money was after he saw a photo on my social media. I explained that if he felt it was necessary, he should go through the Child Maintenance Service instead. CMS later confirmed that my income was too low for payments and, more importantly, that the time our daughter spends with me is significant. It felt like that whole obsession with holding a tiny majority of nights finally fell apart. I always saw it as unfair, a deliberate form of control designed to gain financial benefits. Seeing it in black and white was a quiet relief. It proved the truth and gave me room to breathe.

When the judge rejected Mauricio's request to take our daughter to another country and to be granted full custody, I remember he encouraged us to talk and make decisions based on what was truly best for her. He said he did not want to impose a resolution, because he trusted that, as parents, we would be able to recognise what was in our daughter's best interest. Mauricio and I have gradually come to accept that it is, in fact, better for her to spend more time with me.

But spending more time with my daughter has never been about money; it has always been about giving her the greatest possible comfort, safety and opportunities. It is sad when financial interests are placed above healthy co-parenting, and used as an excuse to ignore a child's real needs or to silence their voice or the voice of the other parent.

Looking back I can see how clearly Mauricio always showed signs of choosing any route that would save him from spending money. Whether it was bargaining with the Marias in my hometown; going to a restaurant with family and friends and then handing out vouchers to everyone at the table to get a free meal, or even expecting to be upgraded to first class just by wearing a fancy suit at the airport. If there was any chance to get something for free, he would take it. I still remember the embarrassment I felt when he insisted on getting a refund at Shoe Zone because the soles of our daughter's shoes came off a year after we'd bought them. He had kept the receipt and used one of his favourite phrases: 'the customer is always right'. Mauricio would go to any length just to save a bit of money.

Living on a boat to avoid paying rent, limiting our daughter's basic needs to save money, and using her pocket money from birthdays or Christmas to 'teach her a lesson' are just a few examples of the choices Mauricio sees as normal.

Whenever I raise these concerns, especially when they affect our daughter's hygiene, nutrition, and emotional wellbeing, Mauricio accuses me of being controlling. He fails to see the impact this kind of authority and financial control has on our daughter, or the harm it causes her.

He recently came up with the idea of enrolling our daughter to a private school in central London. Assuring me that he 'had a way', and that 'it wouldn't cost me anything', but refused to say how. It turned out he was hoping that our daughter would get a scholarship, though only a tiny fraction of applicants actually get one. It is not that I did not believe our daughter was talented, I just wanted to be realistic about what we could afford and what was best for her. With him, things always feel more complicated than they need to be. During this time, he pushed our daughter to study for the first test, but every week I could see how the illusion our daughter once had to get into that school was slowly vanishing. 'He spoiled it for me', she said the night before the exam as we were cycling back home. In the end, she did not get through to the second stage, but to be honest, neither of us felt too upset about it.

It never ceases to surprise me what Mauricio can come up with. A few years back we organised a birthday party for our daughter, and it randomly hailed on that day. I remember seeing Mauricio and our daughter arriving at the party, he was cycling and she was holding on to him, sitting on the bicycle rack just to avoid paying for a cab.

Pushing our daughter to her physical limits has become almost like an obsession for Mauricio: making her walk long distances carrying her own backpack at a very young age, expecting her to cycle far distances everyday, training in martial arts twice per week after school, leaving her exhausted. Her feelings were just disregarded. She was told to just keep up and perform. The moment when everything broke for her was when Mauricio repeatedly ignored basic safety boundaries and forced her to do something she clearly did not want to. These activities, presented as accomplishments, have too often disregarded her boundaries and comfort, leaving her feeling fearful instead of confident.

Whenever I tried to rationalise with Mauricio and pleaded for some compassion for our daughter, my concerns were always dismissed. It was only when I involved third parties, that Mauricio would show a more reasonable response. For example, when I raised my concerns at school about our daughter's extracurricular activities, Mauricio was more reasonable and agreed that she should drop some activities that were clearly too much for her during the week. Similarly, when I expressed my worries in front of a third party, about the training our daughter was receiving, Mauricio agreed to postpone the certification for a few years as long as I paid him back what he had already spent. But then, went behind my back and organised it anyway.

I cannot ignore how these disputes have become a twisted and exhausting way of keeping me tied to Mauricio through conflict, rather than allowing me to move forward freely. Over the years, I have noticed a clear pattern: after particularly hurtful comments or dismissive behaviour towards me, Mauricio often sends a "token" through our daughter. She would come home with things like a handmade bird feeder, toys for my son, or even treats for our dog. Although these may seem like small, harmless gestures, to me they are attempts to maintain an indirect connection, an unresolved emotional thread that I am no longer willing to entertain.

In a surprising turn of events, Mauricio expressed bewilderment at my newfound assertiveness and refusal to be undermined as a mother. Little does he know, this transformation stems from a deep-seated sense of worthiness and empowerment that has blossomed within me. Gone are the days of tiptoeing around conflict or acquiescing to his presumptions of superiority. I now stand firm in the knowledge that I, too, am right, and I refuse to allow him to dictate the narrative any longer.

I am fully committed to protecting my children, always putting their emotional and physical well-being first, because this is part of my soul's mission: to give them a safe, stable, and loving home where they feel heard, cared for, and free.

Looking back, it is clear to me now that every challenge I faced—every test—was part of a larger lesson, designed to prepare me for where I stand today. The synchronicities and messages from my guides illuminated the purpose of my journey, giving me faith in a brighter future when I thought everything was lost.

Each hardship demanded consistent effort, and each time, I rose to meet it, learning something invaluable along the way. Whether it was managing the logistics of raising two children on my own or facing sudden, difficult moments, every challenge tested me. Like that morning after I was unexpectedly left alone at home, I had no choice but to find the strength to get my daughter to school. These experiences forced me to tap into a resilience and resourcefulness I hadn't realised I possessed.

Though my finances are still recovering and I carry the weight of debt, I've reached a place where I feel more financially independent. By balancing part-time work with my full-time job as a mum, I've begun to rebuild my financial stability. But more than that, this path has allowed me to reconnect with my true self. Without the presence of Steve, I had the space to rediscover who I was and to make choices that align with my passions and values.

It was time for me to make my own heart full, to pour love into myself until it overflowed. And this meant recognising that the love I was craving from

Steve: the validation, the care, was actually the love I needed to give to myself.

By truly embracing this, I learnt to let go. Not just of the relationship, but of the resentment and hard feelings that came with it. Letting go allowed me to step into a new era, one where I no longer perpetuate the unhealthy dynamics that had followed me for so long. I am in control of my reality now, and I know that I have the power to make myself happy.

To truly be happy, I had to step up for myself. I had to take responsibility for my own needs: financial, emotional, and personal. I had to learn not to rely on anyone else, especially not a man.

Ironically, the financial independence I sought came from the hardships Steve's departure had forced upon me. My original plan had been to stay home with my children until our son turned three and started nursery, but with no money to pay rent, I was forced to find a job. Within two months of Steve leaving, I had secured an online tutoring job, working just a few hours a week. But this job opened the door to work that aligned with my passions for science and helping young people, allowing me to be a dedicated mother while focusing on something I enjoyed.

Over time, I started to build my professional life as a private tutor. My clients began to seek me out, drawn by the results I was achieving with their children. Word of mouth spread, and I received glowing recommendations that filled me with pride. More than that, I felt I was becoming an active and appreciated member of my community. Through voluntary work, I found a deeper sense of purpose, knowing that the women and young people I worked with valued the support I offered.

Being left to fend for myself was undeniably challenging, but it also became a catalyst for growth. Each obstacle I faced was an opportunity to align more deeply with my true self, building piece by piece, a life on my own terms. Just as Merlin predicted, with the crumbling of the Tower I was called to reconstruct my life and be where I *wanted* to be, not where I *had* to be.

I was called to deeply declutter our home, every corner, every single drawer and cupboard. It became a physical reflection of what I was doing within myself. I remember how I had organised everything except for one area: a shelf meant for my work. I had neglected it, and it stood as a symbol of the order I needed in my professional life. By facing that small challenge, I began making a conscious effort to give the love, attention, and energy I had so freely given to others back to myself.

Building my life on my own terms also meant making more intentional decisions about the things I brought into our home, whether food or clothing. Unlike Mauricio, who always went for the cheapest option regardless of quality and considered paying for food a waste of money, I chose to invest in high-quality products. Not because of a brand name, but because I saw it as an investment in myself and in my children. I became more thoughtful in my purchases, buying only what was truly needed and ensuring that what I did choose was of good quality.

This shift brought a visible change to our home. The house began to look and feel different, and I felt a quiet pride in the transformation. When guests commented on how lovely everything looked, I knew it was a reflection of the care I was now putting into my life. My daughter noticed it too, she pointed out how our plants were blooming and how our orchid was 'going wild.' That moment meant a lot to me. Orchids had always been difficult for me to keep alive, no matter what I did. But the one I bought for myself on my birthday three years ago is still thriving.

I also started surprising myself with simple, nourishing acts of self-care. I began preparing meals that weren't just quick fixes, but thoughtful, beautiful dishes that felt good to eat. I was nurturing myself in ways I never had before. Sitting at the table to enjoy a nice meal alone no longer felt wrong. Instead, it became something I looked forward to: colourful, balanced, healthy mains followed by lush desserts and a few cups of tea, just to please myself and no one else.

This sense of investment in myself wasn't just material, it extended to my physical and mental well-being. I rediscovered my passion for bouldering, which I had loved before getting pregnant with my son. Back then, I used to go with a close friend, but since I can no longer afford the family membership, I take my kids to the boulders in Fairlop or spend a few minutes on the climbing wall near my daughter's school, making the most of the free access to something that makes me feel strong and alive.

I came to appreciate how much physical activity was helping me. The tension in my back and the aches that had plagued me started to disappear, and I noticed the tingling in my body as a reminder to keep going. Exercise became more than a way to stay fit. It became a way to regulate my emotions and clear my mind. It was something I did not just for myself, but for my family, too, strengthening us all. My kids developed a love for climbing, and I'm constantly amazed by my daughter's determination as she tackles challenging overhangs. And my son, at just two years old, was already gripping the walls with confidence.

I began to truly feel that I was shedding the old, self-restricting beliefs that had held me back for so long. These beliefs, which had been sabotaging opportunities before they even arrived, have been burned away, leaving me feeling as though I am rising from the ashes like a phoenix. What once seemed impossible now feels within my reach. I've found a new level of confidence, one that has allowed me to embrace my authentic self, follow my passions, and make something meaningful out of them.

A clear realisation emerged through this journey: I am meant to share my experiences. Whether it's teaching science to young people, English to Somali women, or sharing my personal growth story with other women struggling to find love for themselves, I've come to understand that my journey has value. Cat made this clear for me in one of our early sessions, encouraging me to keep a journal and to be 'creative' with my story. She never explicitly said I should write a book, but I chose to do so. Not only to tell my story, but as a way to process my emotions, sit with my feelings, and gain clarity.

It's been cathartic to see how everything is falling into place. The connections I made years ago, along with the new people I've met, have become a reassuring reminder that there was nothing to fear, that the universe had been supporting me all along.

Guided by truth and love, I trust wherever I find myself, I am meant to be there, and that I will find those meant to cross my path. This new mindset opened me up to receiving the blessings life had to offer. I began to let go of control, releasing the beliefs and assumptions that once held me back, and embraced a new self. I opened my mind and heart to what the universe had in store for me.

As I aligned myself with the mindset of trust and self-belief, the pieces of my life began to fall into place, and a profound sense of wholeness emerged. Amazing connections formed effortlessly, each one bringing light, warmth, and a sense of belonging. I found myself surrounded by people who seemed destined to be part of my journey, whether to teach me lessons, offer support, or simply share moments of joy. These connections, woven into the fabric of our daily lives, transformed the logistics of single motherhood into a life filled with gratitude and meaning.

Among these connections, some individuals have truly become cornerstones in my life. My mother, of course, plays a central role, despite being miles away in Mexico. The time difference might separate us, but her ability to tune into my feelings, and even my children's health, has many times left us speechless about her undeniable attune to her maternal instincts. Her worry for me became an unexpected source of motivation, inspiring me to show her that I was doing well. Posting on social media, one positive moment, one good thing I did for myself, became my way of pushing forward. It reassured her and gave me the encouragement I needed to keep moving past negativity.

There's Auntie Jenny, someone I met quite serendipitously. She was a neighbour who also had a dog, and soon enough, she became an integral part of our life at a time when I felt isolated. Her wisdom, maturity, and unconditional support felt like a blessing sent my way, especially when I needed someone to turn to. Before long, she became part of our family. It started with walks in the park, but it grew into something much deeper. Our brunches, quick coffees when I just needed someone to talk to, and those little outings with the kids became part of a meaningful bond that has held strong for the past three years. Jenny always finds ways to make us feel seen and cared for.

There's Auntie Ray, who also supported us to start rebuilding. Her presence brought exactly the kind of energy we needed: warm, dependable, and full of joy. Time with the dogs is always fun, and her care and hard work are truly admirable.

And there's Lee, who first came into our lives helping with Paddy, and then looking after for my son, offering not just practical help but peace of mind when I started tutoring online. I will always hold deep gratitude for her care and loving heart.

I also found quiet strength in the company of other single mothers. We shared stories, worries, and dreams. Each of us navigating motherhood in our own way, yet recognising something familiar in one another. I'm especially grateful for the generosity that passed between us, whether it came as warm meals, shared clothes, or the trust offered in moments of need. These exchanges reminded me that care doesn't always come in grand gestures, it often arrives softly, through simple acts of solidarity. It was also a space for reflection. As we spoke, I could see how differently we each experienced our paths, shaped by our pasts, our perspectives, and our readiness to grow. Those conversations offered both comfort and insight, and they helped me see myself more clearly.

My children and I began to create a rhythm of our own. We felt at ease, safe, at home. And we found warmth and belonging in the places we visited frequently. The familiarity of these local spots, however ordinary, brought a sense of stability and joy that grounded us in our new life. We slowly wove ourselves into the fabric of the neighbourhood, finding comfort in the small rituals of everyday life.

There is Mexican Seoul, our favourite Korean fried chicken spot that is also proudly Mexican, just like me. It is the kind of place that instantly makes you feel at home. Then there is the local fish and chip shop, a family-run business that evolved into a café while staying true to its roots. Café Avenue is a cherished gem, run by people who truly value fairness and kindness. The Approach is a pub managed by good people too, perfect for fish and chips and a pint on a Friday. And the cafés near Victoria Park always offered a well-earned treat after scooting through the park. The ConeFather ice cream van man, with his handmade creations, would always brighten our summers with a treat as we cycled past one of the gates. The Community Centre, where people with lots of incredible stories from their youth connect in a meaningful way with the park. And the Baby Hub at St James the Less at the church around the block, where I met other mums that became good friends.

We've embraced a space of warmth and ease. There's a certain energy that brings a sense of connection. All within two blocks, like my ancestors kept telling Cat in one of our readings. It's something unexpected, yet deeply reassuring. This is exactly where I want to be, surrounded by the people who truly matter. And at the same time, this is where I am meant to be.

◆ ◆ ◆

Chapter 6

Embracing Wholeness as a Family

In caring for my children, I began to rediscover the version of myself I had abandoned: someone capable, resilient, and deserving of love. And as the cards foretold, my children would serve as the grounding force in my life, keeping me rooted in reality while also empowering me to soar to new heights. Coming to London was always part of my destiny, to raise my children and reclaim my power. Our love became the greatest strength, guiding us through the darkest of times and illuminating the path to healing and renewal.

I suddenly found myself entrenched in habits that didn't align with my true self. I realised the need to reinvent our routines, both for my son and for our entire family. Prioritising his needs had come at the expense of everyone else's comfort. So, I set about rearranging the layout of our home to create an environment that catered to the needs of all family members, including my daughter and our dog.

I saw the importance of reclaiming simple yet meaningful traditions, such as family dinners without the distraction of television. Watching TV during dinner had become a habit, but it hindered our ability to connect. I reinstated the tradition of enjoying dinner as a time for conversation, providing a space for us to share talk and plan for the next day. This seemingly small change has had a profound impact on our family dynamic, fostering a greater sense of focus, connection, and well-being for myself and my children. Now we can also enjoy moments of laughter and hold meals with our guests since something as simple as clearing the dinner table has been changed. I've come to realise how I had unknowingly been making things more difficult and tedious for myself, but by making intentional changes, I've found greater ease and fulfilment in our daily lives.

Establishing routines that worked for everyone became paramount, leading to the creation of a weekly calendar ensuring that each day, my three babies: my son, my daughter, and our beloved dog received attention and care. Managing their schedules required finding practical and affordable solutions.

Cycling quickly became another unexpected source of connection and strength for our family. Initially a necessity to manage school drop-offs, it evolved into a cherished family activity. At six months, there was no other option but to take my son on the cycle rides for the school drop offs, although I was worried he might be uncomfortable, he was immediately delighted in the speed and movement, often gesturing for me to go faster or to keep moving. His presence made our rides even more joyful. His love for riding has only grown and he's now a master of his trike and his scooter.

The cycling rides became moments of shared resilience and joy, bonding us in ways I hadn't anticipated. With my daughter, the relaxed pace of cycling encouraged meaningful conversations. The rhythm of pedalling, pausing for pedestrians, and the gentle flow of movement created a safe space to open up about our thoughts and feelings. It became a shared experience that bonded us and revealed our inner strength.

We became an active and adventurous family. Part of it felt divinely guided. Cat said in one of the first readings that it was good for me and my kids to stay connected with nature and because of her advice, I booked a sound healing ceremony for myself in Epping Forest. On that trip, I discovered that by simply taking the Central Line, we could get all the way to Epping Forest or to Fairlop, without having to make any changes or get on a bus. I remember thinking 'if only I could take the buggy down those steps' to get to the underground. That night, as I was laying in bed, I thought I could tilt up the front tyre of the buggy on our way down the stairs, carefully sliding down the two back tyres of the buggy at the same time, our Mountain Buggy had the perfect wheels for that. I was sure I could hold on to that buggy, making sure to keep my boy safe. I wanted to do it. I was going to do it.

The next day, I took the kids to that forest. The steps to get the buggy on the central line were not an obstacle for us. I could manage the buggy on the stairs on my own. Counting out loud our way down, while my son was sitting patiently, listening, step by step. My daughter carried our dog on the escalator and everything was fine. Anytime we wanted, we could get on any train to get to school, or to dance, or to Fairlop, or to the forest. Each time, my son would marvel about the train tracks or the passing trains, pretending that he is driving the train, melting our hearts with his sweet innocence.

We can get anywhere walking, using our bikes, scooters, or the train. Any obstacle, any new challenge, just required determination, patience and resilience. I remember how frustrating those trips felt at the beginning, as if I was fighting something in myself. I was overriding the old habits and beliefs and part of me was scared. I wanted to believe that I could do it but I was afraid of letting go. But every challenge I overcame was just proof of how much I was capable of. Time after time, doing my best, acting in good faith, showing what I am made of, the values I had and what I wanted to teach to my kids. It was only through them that I was able to find the best version of myself, an unconditional love coming from within for them. So I could jump, to bridge the gap.

Even in face of adversity, there was always something to be grateful for. Surprises, blessings and gifts never ceased to appear. It was almost as if by doing the right actions, as small as clearing a drawer, the right outcome would come. I still find objects that I have been thinking of after randomly feeling called to clean a shelf or a cabinet. Just a few days ago, I was at Sainsbury's trying to decide if I should buy the extension lead they had for eight pounds, and I wasn't sure. The size was too big, and the price was a bit much. It didn't feel right so I did not get it. That evening, I dropped a pencil near a corner and when I picked it up, I noticed some dust behind some toys nearby and as I was tidying up that corner, there was a spare extension lead I had forgotten about. It was the perfect size, just what I had thought of earlier that morning.

This journey has been a mission, of empowerment, to recognise the value of our voice, and to take guided actions led by our inner truth. My path of transformation has shown me how to trust my instincts and honour my story. And through it all, I've learned to see every blessing, no matter how small or symbolic, as proof that we were always guided and protected.

I remember that for our first winter, we had to go to the baby bank at a church in Hackney to get clothes for my son. Although it rarely snows in London, it had snowed the night before making the roads icy. The quest was extra hard. When my son and I arrived, I showed my completed registration form online and they gave us two very thoughtful, and very heavy, prepackaged packs of clothes for my son. They also said I could get one coat for each of my children from the clothes rack in the room next door. When we went inside, there were other mums that had arrived first, and they were all gutted because two particular coats from the rack did not fit their children. When I had a look, they were the exact sizes we needed, and they happened to be from a designer brand. I remember friends commenting on the fancy coats, and I always told them they came from the baby bank at the church. But when my daughter asked me, I simply said I bought them because I didn't want her to feel different or worried.

Little things like that kept happening but I didn't see before that it was God showing us unconditional love and abundance. The Universe sending kind hearted people our way. All this time, to give us a hand. My son's godparents would always surprise us with the most thoughtful gifts or memberships; friends would show up with bundles of clothes or food; and even one time, Jenny had 'accidentally ordered too much food' and needed to make some space in her cupboards, and decided that the solution was to give us all that food. She came with a full trolley, restocking our fridge for a week, without knowing it was at the time we needed it the most. And even a good friend organised and paid for us a breathtaking holiday in the Alps during last summer, allowing us to experience something we could have never afforded on our own.

It feels like even strangers have been divinely guided to help us in some way. I remember a random lady standing near the toilets by the Pavilion, waving at me, asking if I wanted to take a loaf of bread and some muffins they hadn't been able to sell on that day. Even furniture would lay on the streets for us to take home. There was a time when I was taking my son to an appointment at the children's centre. Just down our road there was a children's kitchen on the street for someone to take, but I thought to myself that it didn't seem so nice and that I was in a rush anyway. On our way home the kitchen was gone. A few days later, a bigger and nicer kitchen appeared for my son. People complement it when they visit, and they are in disbelief when I tell them we found it. A rocking horse, doll's houses, and bookshelves spread around the house reminding us how lucky we are. There was the side table my daughter and I had casually discussed needing, which magically appeared next to the bins in our building the very next day.

Just a few months ago, my daughter asked me if I could get her more books of the Alex Rider collection and the very next weekend, as I visited one of my students, her mum said she had been tidying up and she had some books and clothes I could take. There were seven Alex Rider books, neatly arranged, waiting for me to take home. Last year, I received a tax refund that turned out to be an overpayment by HMRC. As soon as they notified me of the error, I cooperated fully and explained that I had always declared my finances honestly. I was transparent about my situation and, given my limited means, we agreed on a fair repayment plan spread over three years, which I am currently following.

These synchronicities and gifts were the materialisation of Cat's promise during my first reading with her: 'You and your kids will always be provided for'. Small gestures from spirit, as a reward for the challenges overcome. Blessings would always come my way. Just in the right moments. Patterns in numbers, symbols and songs presented themselves, bringing a beautiful meaning to our existence. Time and again, I was reminded that we were loved.

I came to understand that as long as I did my part, everything would be ok. That meant taking small steps each day, one after the other towards happiness. I had things to do, places to visit, and two wonderful children that needed me so I could not rely on excuses anymore. I could not blame the rain, the cold, the lack of sleep or the lack of money. With determination and creativity, I could make this work.

Part of that creativity showed up in the little things, like always having snacks ready for the kids. Other mums would often praise how organised we were, admiring the neat containers and healthy options. But the truth is, it wasn't about being a super mum. I simply couldn't afford prepackaged snacks anymore. So on the weekends, I would prepare batches of yoghurt pots with oats and frozen fruit, and stock up on big bags of nuts, fresh fruit, and blocks of cheese. My kids got used to enjoying simple, wholesome snacks. They came to expect homemade sandwiches with their favourite fillings: smoked salmon, cream cheese, sliced cucumber and rye bread were always a hit. Or they would happily munch on berries, dried mango and apple slices, or cubes of cheese on the way home from school.

By saving on snacks, we could start treating ourselves along the way. That meant we could stop for something special on our weekly trips to the woods or to Fairlop, with enough tucked away for a proper meal before catching the train home. That's how we began discovering little hideaways scattered across London.

Stopping by for oysters at the farmer's market after my son's football became a tradition. The kids would always be excited about who would eat more oysters that weekend. We started allowing ourselves to explore the city and indulge in delicious food. Eating together, enjoying good food, nourishing our bodies and souls is now a tradition.

I've always loved that in Korea, people say 'mani meogeoyo', which means 'eat a lot', before a meal. I can't help but smile each time I see my son confidently eating noodles with his chopsticks, or my daughter lighting up as I serve her favourite mul-naengmyeon. They're not afraid to try new flavours, textures, or dishes from different cultures. Their refined palates often surprise people, especially when they ask for sushi or dip their mandu into soy sauce with perfect technique. They'll dip crusty bread into the broth from mussels and happily share a whole kilo between them. Even when we stumble upon something unfamiliar at a market or a new café, they approach it with curiosity and excitement. I feel proud, not just of their evolving tastes, but of the openness and appreciation they carry into every bite.

Our connection deepened, even through food. For a long time, this simple pleasure had felt restricted, something my daughter and I quietly cherished on our own. But we've found a way to reclaim it. Simple yet delicious dinners are now a staple at home, and our little escapes, like a spontaneous trip to the shopping mall for boba tea on a random Tuesday, have become small rituals of joy. I began to see that nourishment could also be about comfort, joy, and simple moments of ease in our daily lives.

There was a time when spending money on food was considered wasteful, something to be avoided or even criticised. But I've come to see it differently. Sharing a good meal, trying new flavours, treating ourselves, it's not frivolous. It's connection, it's culture, it's love. And I want my children to know that.

A few times, during school pick-ups, my daughter would notice I hadn't brought anything for myself. She'd look at me with concern and offer to share her food. Sometimes, I wouldn't even buy a boba for myself, just for them. That's when I realised, I was unconsciously teaching her that love meant sacrifice, that looking after others came before looking after yourself. So now, I pack three sandwiches in the snack bag. I get myself a matcha latte when I buy their treats. These small, intentional gestures are my way of saying: I matter too.

It took time to unlearn the belief that care had to be earned, instead of something I was already worthy of.

That shift was subtle but powerful—an act of quiet transformation. I stopped treating my needs as an afterthought and began honouring them as a vital part of what keeps our family grounded.

Recognising my own needs helped me see more clearly the needs of those around me, even the quiet ones, like Paddy. I still remember the first time he tried his new kibble, he could not stop eating. Before that, he'd grown bored of the cheap, low-nutrient food, and I'd often be woken at midnight by the sound of him being sick on the carpet. His poos were runny, his fur always dirty, and the clean-up added extra weight to my already full days. But since switching his food, all those stomach troubles have disappeared. Now, he's so spoiled he expects me to warm up his grain-free, pure meat tin for a few seconds in the microwave, mix it with his fancy kibble, and top it off with a little seaweed to keep his teeth clean. To be honest, I'm happy to do it. He is my furry boy, and he deserves care too.

Through these shared rituals, we have stitched together a sense of belonging that doesn't rely on perfection, but on love, presence, and truth. This is what wholeness looks like for us: a family built from the ground up, nourished in every way that matters.

Chapter 7
Finding Faith

Something began to shift. It started subtly, quietly. I had already accepted that the only way forward was to take small, intentional steps, trusting that if I did my part, things would work out. But what I didn't expect was how clearly the Universe would begin to respond. The signs were everywhere: numbers, dreams, chance encounters, messages arriving at just the right moment. And slowly, I stopped brushing them off as coincidence. There were simply too many. I began to feel held. Not just in my daily routines, but in something far greater. It was as if the more I trusted myself, the more life opened up around me, mirroring my faith with unexpected blessings and reminders that I was no longer walking alone.

One of those reminders came on an ordinary afternoon, while I was washing dishes. A video popped up on my phone with a message that resonated deeply. The speaker suggested that perhaps the reason God hadn't yet sent me 'my person' was because He had something greater in mind—a purpose that needed my full attention. He spoke about the possibility of writing a book, and the words struck me with both amusement and clarity. I had just finished writing Chapters One and Two. As laughter bubbled up from within, I felt a wave of gratitude rush through me. It was as if the Universe itself was nodding in agreement, gently affirming that I was exactly where I needed to be.

Writing my story began as a way to organise my thoughts and make sense of everything that had happened, but it soon became something deeper. It turned into a healing process. As I wrote, I was forced to admit and confront different aspects of myself. The gaps I avoided, the paragraphs I deleted, the parts I left blank, they were all pointing me toward the areas I most needed to face. It became a process of remembering, reminding, and realigning. Sometimes it was too painful, and I stopped writing altogether. But the Universe has a way of gently bringing me back. Of reminding me to stay on course.

Together, these chapters have become a record of transformation. They are evidence of how embracing my inner abundance and surrendering to the unknown allowed me to build a life of wholeness, love, and fulfilment for myself and my family. But reaching this place meant releasing control. I could no longer cling to plans, timelines, or expectations. The more I tried to manage every outcome, the more disconnected I felt from the natural rhythm of life. It was only when I softened my grip, when I began to trust, that I discovered the quiet power of letting go.

Surrendering wasn't about giving up. It was about leaning into faith, faith in myself, in God, and in the journey that had brought me to this moment. This surrender also meant allowing myself to recognise my worth, not as defined by my struggles or achievements but as inherent and undeniable. It was about choosing, again and again, to love myself. To see myself as the amazing, powerful person who had created a life of possibility and abundance for my children. To celebrate the woman who refused to give up, even in the face of immense adversity. I needed to love myself.

Part of that love meant protecting my energy. I became more discerning about where, and with whom, I shared my light. I no longer felt the need to explain myself or justify my choices. I began to recognise when something or someone no longer aligned with who I was becoming. I started to notice the quiet signs: the silence after I shared something heartfelt, the double spaces in a message, the subtle attempts to define what I wanted or assume how I felt, and the way people reacted to what I shared or how I looked, even when I felt radiant, but omitted the praise. I chose peace. I chose clarity. I chose to honour my growth by sharing my light only with those who could truly receive it, without shrinking it, questioning it, or making it about themselves. Recognise my worth.

Sometimes, love also showed up in the smallest, most unexpected ways. A few months back, I began losing a lot of hair after buying the cheapest shampoo and conditioner I could find: two massive bottles from the chemist at a ridiculous price. One day, standing under the shower, I looked at the bottle in my hand and felt something inside me whisper that it wasn't right. But I kept going. Later that day, while walking through the park with the kids, I overheard two very elegant-looking older women talking. They were surprised that a friend of theirs refused to spend money on quality products for herself, and I knew instantly that the message was for me.

That evening, I made a new decision. I ordered a set of handmade organic shampoo bars and, eventually, my daughter and I found a refill shop near her school where we discovered the most beautiful rose-scented shampoo and conditioner. I refilled the old containers, this time with something good. Something nourishing. Taking a shower became more than just a necessity, it became a ritual. A simple, fifteen-minute moment of care and renewal that lifted my spirits and helped me start the day with intention.

Other small rituals followed. Simple things, like sitting down for a proper meal after exercising in the morning, became acts of self-love. I still struggle to remember to eat, and sometimes it isn't until midday, when my stomach starts to ache, that I realise I've only had a cup of tea. It's often my sister's encouragement, 'to eat well, to nurture my body', that reminds me why it matters. I started replacing the biscuits and chocolate with a small box on the dining table filled with compartments of nuts and dried fruit, ready and within reach. My morning matcha latte, carried in my reusable cup, became another gentle offering to myself. I love the flavour, and I tell myself it's good for my skin, but mostly, it's a way of saying: I am worth this.

I also began to realise that keeping myself 'occupied instead of preoccupied,' as my mum always says, made the days lighter. Structure brought calm to my mind. Leaving the house on Mondays or Tuesdays in my leggings, with my climbing shoes packed, became a quiet commitment to myself, a way to make sure I didn't return home and lose momentum. On

Thursdays, after my son's dance class, I used to rush home, hiding under a jumper I'd worn for days, avoiding small talk with the other mums. But I decided to change. On days I wasn't climbing, I made myself shower, put on lipstick and clean clothes. That simple effort changed everything. I felt more open, more confident, more present.

The version of me that once hid away out of shame or exhaustion was slowly, gently being replaced by someone ready to be seen, someone embracing life with vitality, love, and faith. I had come to understand that my presence in the world carried meaning and purpose. I had a role to play in something far greater than I could yet comprehend.

In the evenings, tidying the house became a quiet ritual, part winding down and part resetting. I would put on a personal development video in the background and move through each step of my routine: starting a laundry load, washing the dishes, folding the clothes from the night before, then hanging the freshly washed ones to dry, and finally wiping the floor. This repetition, once draining, became grounding. It created ease for the mornings to come.

I made small, intentional changes that had a big impact: separate baskets for different types of laundry, a robot vacuum, a dish rack over the sink. Slowly, the sense of being buried under endless tasks began to fade. I no longer felt suffocated by the invisible weight of it all. I created space, not just physical, but mental. Space where I could sit down and write, or even watch an episode of the series I had chosen just for me.

One night, I watched a documentary about the Blue Zones, regions of the world where people live the longest, and learned about the health benefits of deep squatting. It reminded me of my Korean roots, where squatting close to the ground is still part of everyday life: for cooking, cleaning, even resting. Inspired by that, I began to clean my floors in a deep squat, using a small hand brush I keep in the hallway, followed by a damp cloth. This act became both a stretch and a prayer, a way to care for my body while tending to the home I share with my children. It felt ancestral, almost ceremonial.

With that space came clarity. I began to shape my own narrative. I began to choose the thoughts I allowed in, to rewrite the stories I'd been told. I leaned into a mindset of love and fulfilment. Even my social media feeds began to reflect that shift. I started receiving more content focused on healing, abundance, and spiritual growth. Some of the messages were subtle; others felt undeniably direct.

Finding support through a debt advice service was another act of self-love and trust. And when a series of unexpected payments and gifts arrived, I took it all as a sign: a new start. A message from the divine. A reward for entering a new era, one rooted in blessings, balance, and love.

There was a shift in everything, as if I had become someone entirely new. Little things that once felt heavy now carried light. Even the topics that caught my attention during those evening resets no longer revolved around dissecting my past, but celebrating who I am and what I'm capable of. I was releasing shame, anger, betrayal, abandonment, hardship. I was no longer trying to make sense of the pain. I was living beyond it.

As I write these words, Take Me to Church is playing on my phone. I haven't called myself religious since I started secondary school, but this journey—this rebirth—has been filled with signs, meaning, and purpose for my soul. And now, it's time to take God within me. To let that presence move through my choices, my healing, my voice. To act from faith, because I am the protagonist of my own story. Held, always, by unconditional love.

Even the most unexpected moments became reminders. We laughed when I got raffle ticket number 69 at Jenny's party last year, but with time, it became symbolic of love for me. Not in the way I imagined, but in the way I needed. I've come to understand that my relationships will always mirror the relationship I have with myself. I can only truly connect with someone else when I am connected with me. I can only receive real love when I'm ready for it.

One day, I got a playful nudge from the universe. I was about to take our dog out when a video started playing on my phone. The speaker said, 'Some of you want to meet the right person, but if you ran into them on the street today, you wouldn't give the right impression.' I looked at my reflection in the mirror: pyjama bottoms, messy hair, and no intention of changing. And I laughed. Really? I thought. Is this how you're going to meet The One today?

So I changed. I swapped the pyjama bottoms for jeans, brushed my hair, put on a beanie and some lipstick, making me feel a little bit more prepared. It wasn't about impressing anyone. It was about respecting the version of myself that was showing up for life. And I began to notice that the more I focused on myself, the more connected I felt, even to the love I hadn't met yet. Loving myself, like eating well after climbing to take care of my body, was a way of preparing to receive love. 'Train like you're getting ready for Henry Cavill to feel it,' said a video I was watching after I made myself a bibimbap after training. That was motivation enough. If I showed up as my best, looking and feeling like myself, maybe I'd be ready when love arrived.

But if I'm being honest... I wasn't ready. Not fully. Deep down, I knew there were still things trying to rise to the surface. And I couldn't keep ignoring them.

I still caught myself in self-sabotaging patterns. Moments of self-doubt, distraction, and fear. I'd get ready in the morning and lose track of time, then run late, frustrated with myself. Sometimes I avoided going out unless it was for the kids. I dreaded small talk. I felt overwhelmed when there were too many people at the door. And there were times I walked past a shop instead of going in. I've even caught myself wondering if strangers laughing in the street were laughing at me, mentally listing all the things they might be criticising. Only to realise they weren't even looking in my direction. These moments have become humbling reminders: those fears are just in my mind. And they don't get to define me.

That same quiet truth came to me when I thought about quitting smoking. For over a year, it had become part of my evening routine, a ritual I barely questioned. Once the kids were asleep and the house was quiet, I would step onto the balcony and light a cigarette, as if it were my moment to breathe. It gave me the illusion of control, of release, but deep down, I knew it wasn't serving me.

A few months ago, I had a sore throat that lingered for two full weeks. I knew, instinctively, that it was the smoking. But I ignored it, hoping it would pass. The discomfort stayed, and eventually I stopped noticing it. I adapted to the ache, as if that was the price I had to pay to cope. Then one day, a reel appeared on my phone. It showed the damage smoking does to the alveoli in your lungs. I kept watching. The next video was about someone who had quit smoking and found a deeper connection to God. And something in me stirred. I felt the invitation.

I wanted to try. And I did. I made it three days.

That night, I felt the urge again. I stepped out onto the balcony with a cigarette in hand, looking up at the stars and scrolling through videos. And then, a woman's voice: 'Remember, there is a last task for you. You need to pray—and FAST.' And I knew. She wasn't talking about food. So I had to try again. To fast from what no longer serves me. To choose myself. To start over, this time, with full intention. A new beginning in every way.

With determination, I gathered the entire box of cigarettes, and tossed it out altogether, symbolising my commitment to free myself from my addictions and truly care for every part of who I am.

After that act of release, I went to bed. As I checked the time, it was exactly 2:22 AM on the 22nd of February, 222 222. That precise moment felt like a divine confirmation, a clear sign that I was on the right path. In that instant, I knew that every step towards transformation was drawing me closer to a fuller version of myself, ready to embrace the genuine connection that destiny has in store.

Letting go of my addictions and taking some time on my own, created the space I needed to transform. I became more comfortable in my own company. I could sit with my emotions, acknowledge my feelings, and listen to my intuition without trying to escape or numb them. The clarity was almost immediate. My dreams became more vivid, more powerful. And my inner knowing sharpened. It felt like something sacred had been unlocked in me.

I feel this most strongly at night, when the house is quiet and my children are asleep. I'll be tidying up, and suddenly I'm pulled into their rooms, only to find one of them overheating under the blankets, or curled too close to the edge of the bed. That instinctive knowing has always been there. My mother has it too with me and my sister. But what's even more incredible is the way her connection extends to my children. She will message me out of the blue to ask if my daughter's stomach is hurting, or if my son needs cough medicine, and somehow, it always aligns with what they're going through.

Her intuition is only one part of the story. Her dreams have always acted as portals: bringing messages of love and protection from our ancestors, from my grandparents and great-grandparents. Growing up, she was the one who dreamt of premonitions. Even when I kept things secret, she would dream of symbols, places, or people that mirrored my inner world, offering guidance I hadn't dared to ask for.

For a long time, I believed that gift belonged to her alone. But something shifted in me over the past two years. I began to have dreams of my own, about my grandparents, my children, even about a lover. Dreams that carried clear messages: to make a choice, to keep going, to trust that a reward was coming. These weren't just dreams, they were transmissions. And since giving up smoking, that connection has deepened. It's as if I now sleep with the door open to a realm I was once too clouded to access.

And then, during the portal, when the planetary alignments were said to open new pathways, something powerful happened. I had just come back from a hypnotherapy session, one I had unknowingly booked at the perfect time, on the perfect day, as if something greater had arranged it for me. I was already in a space of openness, realignment, and surrender.

That night, something shifted. I crossed into a deeper knowing. It happened in a dream, but it felt more like an experience than a vision. In the dream, I was holding my son in my arms. His small body was warm against me, his breathing a little heavy. I brought my hand to his nose and, using my thumb and index finger, I gently squeezed and slid everything that was stuck downwards. I didn't just see it, I felt it. I felt the suction, the release, the way his nostrils cleared, as if I had really been there, helping him breathe with my own hands.

When I woke, I felt certain that my baby was better. I didn't message his father. I didn't need to. Later that day, Steve said, 'He's feeling much better now.' But I already knew.

I wasn't just stepping into a new phase in my life, I was stepping into new power. It has always been there, this knowing, this connection between mothers and their children. And it's not just me. For centuries, we've been told that we are imagining things, that intuition is just a feeling, that our knowing is unreliable. But I am done with that lie.

Because my mother knew, and now I know, and so does my daughter. Because I now understand, with absolute certainty, that we women are capable of so much more than we've been told. The more we trust that, the more powerful we become.

Two nights later, without planning it, I found myself helping my daughter through my dreams as well. This time, I was on a diving trip with her, making her feel relaxed, cared for, and safe. I could see her radiant smile and golden hair, curled from the water. When we stopped at one of the islands, my grandfather as a younger man, joined us. He rested on the couch beside us, offering his company and protection. It was as if we were released from the heavy darkness Mauricio had once placed on us.

And then, another dream came to me, reminding me of a choice I made thirteen years ago: to leave my home country with a man I barely knew. In the dream, a humble-looking man offered me a ride on his motorbike from my hometown to where I was meant to meet my children. We arrived at a beautiful lake, surrounded by mountains. As we stopped, he looked at me and said, 'Guatemala wasn't a bad choice after all.' And I realised that the path that followed that choice had led me to the most precious gifts of all: my children. It has always been my destiny to heal for children. Because true love pushes you to question your reality, how you have lived your life, and challenges you to take action. It calls you to be courageous and speak your truth. Trust your intuition.

With each passing day, I see more and more signs that reaffirm my path, of healing, growth, and authenticity. As I bask in the warmth of gratitude and spiritual connection, I am filled with hope for a future brimming with endless possibilities and boundless love. I feel a profound sense of contentment and clarity, knowing that I am exactly where I need to be, guided by the divine. I've come to realise that this journey has been a lesson for my soul, one that has revealed the power within me all along.

For so long, I had looked for what I needed outside myself, but now I understand that the light and healing I sought were always inside. I needed a trigger for my spiritual awakening, something to help me bridge the gap between the life I had and the life I was meant to live. And in this moment of clarity, I was finally able to embrace happiness and self-love. I began to see myself as the vessel that channels the prosperity and love my children and I deserve. To create, to live authentically, and to follow my passions with confidence.

My own healing has also opened the door for my daughter to begin her own healing. After the day I was attacked, she developed an irrational fear of cloudy days, as she related my bruises to the clouds. For months, she feared I would be hurt again. She never saw what happened to me, but all she saw were the bruises on my body when I was in the shower. Later, a friend suggested I tell her the truth about how I was hurt and who had hurt me. After I did, her fear disappeared. It was almost as if by speaking the truth, I set her free. By talking about it instead of ignoring it, we made ourselves powerful together, showing her the strength in confronting the truth.

In the months that followed, I made the conscious choice to teach my daughter what it means to trust her intuition. To express her voice. To say no when something doesn't feel right.

We had a neighbour, an old creepy man, who lived in the flat next door. Every time he passed by our window, he would slow his steps, turn his head, and look inside. When I stood at the sink doing the dishes, I could see him watching, lingering, making me feel exposed in my own home. I didn't want him looking into our space, I didn't want that feeling of intrusion anymore. So I did something about it. I ordered window covers so no one could see through. And when my daughter asked why, instead of brushing it off or sugarcoating it, I told her the truth. 'Because I want our privacy,' I said. 'Because I don't want that man looking inside.'

For so long, we had been told not to talk about things like this. To ignore them, suppress them, pretend they aren't happening. But I refused to teach my daughter that silence was the answer. I wanted her to know that she has the right to say no, to protect her space, to honour what feels wrong. That moment was a small shift, but one that mattered.

Then, another test of my boundaries arose. I was with my son, waiting for the lift at the foot tunnel in Greenwich. As the doors opened, a man and his wife stepped out, but just before he walked past me, I heard the distinct click of a camera. I saw the way he carried it in front of him. And in an instant, I knew what had happened.

Before, I might have hesitated. I might have felt a rush of adrenaline, my heartbeat racing as I questioned myself, as I swallowed my discomfort. But this time, I didn't hesitate at all. I turned to him and said, 'Excuse me.' He stopped. And I watched as he instinctively looked at his camera, opened the picture, saw my bright red coat in the frame, and without me even saying it, he deleted it.

'Thank you,' I said. And I walked away.

I didn't feel fear, I didn't feel doubt. I felt satisfied. Clear. Certain. I had spoken up, set a boundary, and reclaimed my own presence.

Another day, I was leaving my building, dressed up, feeling good, heading to a party. The creepy neighbour was standing near the lift, waiting for the rest of his family, who were still at their door. He called the lift and, when it arrived, he turned to me and said, 'Come in.' But I didn't want to. I didn't want to be inside a small, enclosed space with him. I didn't owe him my presence, my compliance, my silence.

So I simply said, 'I'd rather not.' And I took the stairs. Since that day, his family stopped greeting me, stopped saying hello. And I couldn't care less. Because that moment wasn't about them, it was about me. It was about choosing myself over social politeness, about choosing my own comfort over making someone else feel at ease.

For too long, we have been taught to accept things that feel wrong. To make excuses for them. To convince ourselves that we are overreacting, that we should stay quiet, that we should smile and comply. But not anymore.

During our Easter holiday this year, my daughter and I had some of the most heartfelt conversations we've ever shared. Paris felt like a magical place where we could speak openly and safely about what we had both been experiencing. Making me feel a deep sadness for what she had been enduring, and an overwhelming sense of awe at her strength as she was finding a way through it.

It was along the Seine where we realised something: each of us had been questioning ourselves, doubting our own reality, because of the way Mauricio made us feel. When we finally named it out loud, she looked at me and said, "Thank you for telling me this. Now I know I'm not crazy. Now I know I'm not making this up." Her words filled me with grief because she had been living the same thing I had tried to escape from.

This trip was about reclaiming our clarity. It was about preparing ourselves, not for hardship, but for beauty. For joy. We chose to go to lovely places, to eat delicious food, to treat ourselves with tenderness.

Before our daughter was born, Mauricio took me and my family there, and instead of letting us enjoy the city the way we wanted, he put all sorts of restrictions because he considered any expense a waste of money. Two years ago, he brought our daughter to Paris, to celebrate her birthday, but the same restrictions applied to her. He led her to the same landmarks without ever letting her go inside. They didn't enter museums. They didn't go up the Eiffel Tower. He didn't want to pay for the passes. Everything had to be seen from the outside. Spending money on food was discouraged and they were again only allowed to spend the bare minimum.

So, when I came back, this time with my daughter and my son. I knew our worth. And I knew I would no longer teach my children to believe that joy is something they must earn. This time, we didn't question whether we deserved it. We simply lived it. Every day, we did something meaningful. Something that made us feel alive. And with every act of joy, we peeled off another layer of shame and self-doubt.

And through this unravelling, we began to create a new kind of kindness. One rooted in truth. In trust. In having each other's backs. And while there is still a deep, undeniable connection between my daughter and her father, one that I honour, it no longer defines us. It no longer has power over her. Or over us.

Together, we reclaimed our clarity. We affirmed our truth. And we began to trust, not what others insisted was right, but the quiet voice within us.

She had been feeling scared about an upcoming trip, so I gave her a tiny little Virgin Mary and said, "Take her with you. She'll give you courage during your journey." But later she told me that, instead, the little Virgin had sparked something inside her, something that gave her the strength to say out loud that something didn't feel right. She chose not to go, trusting her own voice.

What followed was more than just a change of plans. It was a sacred moment. She chose herself. Her voice. Her truth. A quiet but powerful act of awakening. A moment of liberation. A sign that generational healing is already happening.

Every time I choose not to retaliate, every time I choose to honour our emotions and protect our peace, I am breaking a cycle. I am showing her what it looks like to walk in dignity, even in the face of manipulation.

For me, for my daughter, for the generations before us who were punished for their instincts, for all the women now stepping into their power, we are done being silent.

We are done second-guessing ourselves. We are done making space for people who take away ours.

And with every step forward, we honour the women who came before us by becoming the women they dreamed we could be.

We are rewriting the story our mothers were never allowed to tell.

Planting seeds of truth in the very soil where silence once grew.

Choosing abundance, gratitude, and curiosity, honouring that quiet inner voice that guides us at every moment.

Acting with good intentions, from a place of love and truth, guided and protected towards the light.

Shine brighter than ever, without ever doubting your voice or your light again, because now you know your worth and your rightful place in the universe.

♦♦♦

The Witch's Tree

Something powerful happened today. Almost as if the past few years had been leading up to this exact moment. I've been showing up for Mariia each week, trying to be there in a way that feels real and meaningful. But this weekend wasn't just about mentoring. It was about showing up fully, in my body, in my courage, in my light.

We climbed ropes and ladders during the Gladiator challenge, clipped into harnesses, pushing past that voice that says, 'You can't.' We stacked crates and stood on top of them, balancing high off the ground, relying on each other not to fall. We walked through mud and crossed rivers, soaked but steady, feeling revitalised by the cold water and the air around us.

There was a quiet strength between us, between Mariia and me. I could feel her seeing me not just as someone helping her, but as someone real. Brave. Present. And I trusted myself in a way I hadn't in a long time.

And then, at the end of it all, we arrived at the Witch's Tree: a birch that has lived more than three times longer than it should. They say a woman was once tied to it. A healer. Someone who understood things others feared. They tried to silence her. But the tree lived. She lived. She didn't just survive, she grew. Tall, rooted, and still standing.

When I touched that part of the trunk where her face seems to appear, it felt... personal. Like she knew me. Like she'd been waiting. I'm not just a mother. Not just someone's past. I'm a woman who can lead. Who can rise. Who can hold space for others and still hold space for herself.

Later, I sat on the hallway steps alone, my legs aching, my heart full. And I remembered: the theme of this trip was 'Step into the gap.' My ancestors have been whispering 'Bridge the gap' for so long. I never fully understood it, until now. But today... I fully stepped in.

Artwork by Mariia Motenko

Epilogue

In the end, I chose to surrender, not out of weakness, but out of strength. I surrendered to the truth, to what is right, and to the quiet power that comes with doing what is best for my children. I no longer carry the burden of proving myself to those who cannot or will not see clearly. Instead, I anchor myself in what is honest, in what brings peace, and in what protects the innocence of those who matter most. Justice, I've learned, begins in the heart, with the decision to act with love, even in the face of injustice.

This story is mine, but it echoes the voices of many who have been silenced. I speak now not out of anger, but out of clarity. I stand not in resistance, but in purpose. To surrender to the truth is to release control and allow what is meant to unfold. And in that surrender, I've found peace. I've found strength. I've found myself.

To all those who have been made to feel like they are not enough

Stay silent.
Be quiet.

These are the words
that I've always heard
Until the day that I finally said no.

No; I will not be quiet.
No; I will not stay silent.
Because every voice, no matter how small,
has the right to be heard.

This is me, and you can never take that from me.
Good luck,
and never forget to speak up.

Poem by Sofia

Artwork by Briony Beech
@the_briony_beech_illustrates

Printed in Dunstable, United Kingdom